D0046814

DEUTSCHE BUNDESPOST BERLIN

CASTLES
A Very Peculiar History™

With added dungeons

'A man's house is his castle.'

Sir Edward Coke
English judge and defender of civil liberty
1552–1643

This book is for Henry.
JM

Editor: Stephen Haynes
Editorial assistants: Rob Walker, Mark Williams
Additional artwork: David Antram, Penko Gelev,
Graham Humphries, John James, Nick Spender,
Rob Walker, Gerald Wood

Published in Great Britain in MMX by
Book House, an imprint of
The Salariya Book Company Ltd
25 Marlborough Place, Brighton BN1 1UB
www.salariya.com
www.book-house.co.uk

HB ISBN-13: 978-1-907184-48-2

© The Salariya Book Company Ltd MMX

5 7 9 8 6 4
A CIP catalogue record for this book is available
from the British Library.
Printed and bound in China.
Printed on paper from sustainable sources.
Reprinted in MMXVI.

Visit our website at **www.salariya.com**
for **free** electronic versions of:
You Wouldn't Want to be an Egyptian Mummy!
You Wouldn't Want to be a Roman Gladiator!
You Wouldn't Want to be a Polar Explorer!
**You Wouldn't Want to sail on a 19th-Century
Whaling Ship!**

WARNING: The Salariya Book Company accepts
no responsibility for the historical recipes in this
book. They are included only for their historical
interest and may not be suitable for modern use.

CASTLES
A Very
Peculiar
History™

With added dungeons

Written by
Jacqueline Morley

Created and designed by
David Salariya

Illustrated by
Mark Bergin

BOOK HOUSE

'They cruelly oppressed the wretched men of the land with castle works; and when the castles were made they filled them with devils and wicked men. Then both by night and day they took those people whom they thought had any goods – men and women – and put them in prison and tortured them.'

An English monk, writing in 1137 of the misdeeds of the Norman barons under weak King Stephen.

'The rich man in his castle,
The poor man at his gate:
God made them high or lowly
And ordered their estate.'

Mrs Alexander, Irish poet and hymn writer
1818–1895

CONTENTS

Putting Castles on the Map

Castles of Great Britain

W Castles

● Other places mentioned in the text

SCOTLAND

Glamis
Stirling
Edinburgh
Berwick-upon-Tweed
Roxburgh
Alnwick
Durham

ENGLAND

Conwy
Penrhyn
Caernarfon
Harlech
Ludlow
Goodrich
Raglan
Gloucester

WALES

Shrewsbury
Bedford
Oxford

Hedingham
Bury St Edmunds
Orford

Rochester
Queenborough
Dover
Bodiam
Hastings

Lacock
Windsor
London
Luscombe
Pevensey

Castle-an-Dinas

Europe and the Middle East

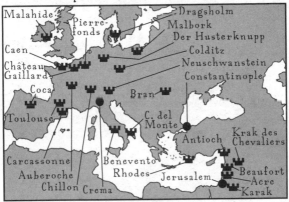

Malahide
Pierre-fonds
Dragsholm
Malbork
Der Husterknupp
Caen
Colditz
Château Gaillard
Neuschwanstein
Coca
Bran
Constantinople
Toulouse
C. del Monte
Antioch
Krak des Chevaliers
Carcassonne
Benevento
Beaufort
Auberoche
Rhodes
Jerusalem
Acre
Chillon
Crema
Karak

Castles of India and Japan

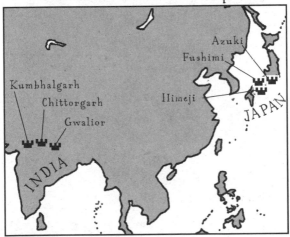

Azuki
Fushimi
Kumbhalgarh
Himeji
Chittorgarh
JAPAN
Gwalior
INDIA

7

Castles Through the Ages

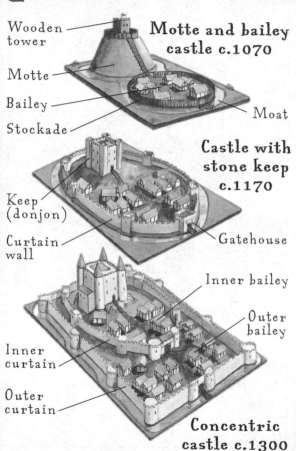

Wooden tower

Motte and bailey castle c.1070

Motte

Bailey

Moat

Stockade

Castle with stone keep c.1170

Keep (donjon)

Curtain wall

Gatehouse

Inner bailey

Outer bailey

Inner curtain

Outer curtain

Concentric castle c.1300

INTRODUCTION

WHAT MAKES A CASTLE A CASTLE?

 e all think we know what a castle is: a big old stone building with battlements, and usually in ruins because people stopped having any use for them ages ago.

But if you'd been living in England around 1050, when it still belonged to the Saxons, you wouldn't have known how to answer. You'd almost certainly never seen a castle – but you'd heard about them, and you didn't like what you'd heard. They were some newfangled type of building that King

Edward the Confessor was letting his French cronies put up on the Welsh borders.

When the king had trouble with his English earls, he'd invited French friends over (he'd been brought up in Normandy) and put them in top jobs. He'd given them land where they'd been putting up private fortifications (they had a French word for them: *chastel* – 'castle'.) And when they were well dug in they'd been riding out and terrorising local people.

That's the definition of a castle. It's the private dwelling of a lord or king, that provides him with a safe, fortified base from which he and his fighting men can keep the upper hand over everyone else in the neighbourhood.

The English monk who recorded the castle-building fad of these foreigners (in his chronicle for the year 1051) had no doubt that it was a bad thing. Saxon and Viking fortifications had been communal efforts, protecting whole towns or settlements against a common enemy. These new castles were private 'me-against-you' affairs. And they had come to stay.

CHAPTER ONE

THE COMING OF CASTLES

astles were the means by which William the Conqueror controlled the English kingdom he had won at the battle of Hastings in 1066. He rewarded the Norman barons who'd backed him by giving them large estates and encouraging them to protect their property – and dishearten the locals – by building castles there. Castles gave you clout. Of course, William granted the land on the strict condition that the barons continued to support him as king and to acknowledge that he was the real owner of the entire country. Over 500 castles sprouted in England during his reign.

WHAT DID THE FIRST CASTLES LOOK LIKE?

At its simplest, a castle was a timber building surrounded by a ditch and an earth rampart. In grander examples, the timber building was a tower set on a man-made mound of earth, called a 'motte'. The top of the mound had a strong fence around it, and its base was protected by the ditch formed when earth was dug out to make the motte.

A wooden bridge linked the motte with a larger enclosure called the 'bailey'. This contained several smaller buildings and also had a surrounding ditch. Earth was piled up on its inner side to form a bank topped by a fearsome row of stakes.

A scene from the Bayeux Tapestry shows soldiers attacking a castle motte.

How to make a Motte

It wouldn't be any good just piling up soil, which would be washed away in the first downpour. You need plenty of hard material well bonded together.

Archaeologists have excavated mottes and found that they were built of alternating layers of different materials, rammed down hard: a layer of soil topped by a layer of stone or shingle, then another layer of soil, and so on.

Steep sides make it difficult for attackers to climb the motte.

Moat (water-filled ditch)

Narrow stairway is easy to defend.

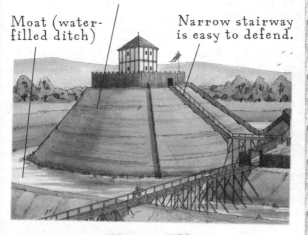

A FLAT-PACK CASTLE?

When William landed on Pevensey beach in Sussex in September 1066, his first concern was to establish a safe base. For this he needed a castle, and quickly. A twelfth-century chronicler says he brought it with him. The writer wasn't an eyewitness, but he may well have been right. It makes sense. When you've just landed in hostile territory you don't want to start felling trees and cutting them to size in full view of the enemy. Shipping precut timbers would save valuable time.

After William's victory at Hastings the people of London took the prudent course and surrendered the city to him. He immediately started a castle there, too. It was the usual earth and timber affair, but within twelve years he had set about replacing it with a massive square tower of stone 27 metres high. It must have seemed a skyscraper to the English, who were used to single-storey wooden buildings.

Building in stone took longer and cost much more than wood, but a stone tower was stronger than a wooden one and made a much more intimidating statement. Stone castles had already appeared on the continent and this was to be the way forward in England too.

The main stone tower of a castle is now called its *keep*, though the Normans called it a *donjon* (which doesn't mean that it was a dungeon, even though it was a good place for holding people prisoner). It provided living quarters for the owner and his family, a safe retreat in times of danger and, above all, a vantage point from which to survey and control the surrounding land.

As a security measure, the entrance to the keep was on the first floor, with a removable wooden stairway outside. The ground floor was used for storage and there were two or three floors of living space above. The first floor was the grand reception hall, which might be divided by a cross-wall into a public hall and a more private chamber. Above were similar rooms for the lord and his family. There were sometimes chambers made in the depth of the walls, which were very thick. Spiral stairs led up and down.

The bailey was crowded with timber buildings, almost like a small village. They housed all the people and activities the castle needed to make sure it could survive without outside help, if necessary: a barracks, an armoury, stables, kennels, blacksmiths' and carpenters' workshops, wagon shed, storage barns, kitchen, brewhouse and bakehouse. There was a large hall where everyone ate together, and a chapel where they heard Mass every day.

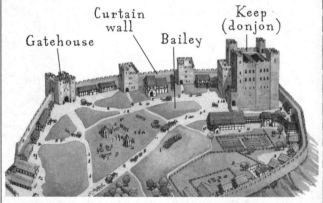

Curtain wall

Keep (donjon)

Gatehouse

Bailey

Rochester castle, Kent, England

The wooden buildings in the bailey have not survived, but this is how they may have looked in the early 13th century.

🅰 CHAPEL STORY

It was everyone's duty to hear Mass in chapel daily, but a certain, very possibly legendary, countess of Anjou, an ancestor of Richard Cœur de Lion, didn't seem to have her heart in it.

She was a woman of great beauty and mysterious charm who would never stay at Mass for the elevation of the Host. When one day her husband tried to force her to stay, she floated out through the chapel window with two of her sons in the folds of her gown, never to return – proof of her devilish origins!

Far from being ashamed of his doubtful ancestor, Richard was proud of her. He boasted of his Anjou family motto:

From the Devil we came; to the Devil we return.

It made a good battle-cry.

William's stone keep at London (now known as the White Tower from its 13th-century whitewashing – quite usual castle practice, to preserve the stonework) was given many additions and had its defences strengthened over the centuries. Richard I added an outer bailey; Henry III extended Richard's bailey with a strong wall and towers; Edward III gave it a second ring of walls.

The Tower has given its name to the whole castle, now Britain's most popular medieval tourist attraction: the Tower of London.

Come and see us some time. You have to pay to get in, but at least it's easier to get out than it used to be...

THE VERSATILE TOWER

At one time or another the Tower of London has been a:

- fortress

- royal palace

- prison

- place of torture and execution

- private menagerie (zoo) (opened to the public in the 18th century, on payment of three halfpence – or of a cat or dog to feed the lions)

- royal mint

- observatory

- record office

- regimental museum

- home of the crown jewels

- top tourist attraction

– and many of these things at the same time.

Although the Tower of London was a functioning castle, with all the usual castle uses, its name always comes with a shudder attached: it spells death on the chopping block! That's because it became the place where traitors were held (Henry VIII found it particularly handy). They went in through Traitors' Gate (the riverside entry) and didn't come out again.

The Tower's first prisoner – but by no means its last – was Ranulf Flambard, bishop of Durham, who was convicted of extortion in 1100. He escaped by climbing down a rope smuggled into his cell in a wine cask.

Lucky Ranulf! Welsh prince Gruffydd ap Llywelyn, who was held in the Tower as a 'guest' of Henry III, didn't do nearly so well. In 1244 he tried to escape down a rope of sheets. His weight was too much for the knots (he was a heavy fellow). They gave way and he fell 27 metres to his death.

⚜FF WITH THEIR HEADS!

If the monarch thought you were dangerous enough to be sent to the Tower for treason, you were probably pretty high-ranking. As such, you were spared a public execution. Among those who enjoyed the privilege of a private beheading within the Tower walls were:

- Anne Boleyn, Henry VIII's second wife, 1536.

- Margaret, Countess of Salisbury, the last of the Plantagenet dynasty, 1541.

- Catherine Howard, Henry's fifth wife, 1542.

- Jane Boleyn, sister-in-law of Anne and involved in Catherine's downfall, 1542.

- Lady Jane Grey, queen of England for nine days, 1554.

- Robert Devereux, Earl of Essex, former favourite of Elizabeth I, 1601.

The last execution at the Tower was that of German spy Josef Jakobs on 14 August 1941, by firing squad.

SERVING A LIFE SENTENCE: THE TOWER OF LONDON RAVENS

For as long as anyone can remember, there have been ravens at the Tower. Their presence is vital for the safety of the UK, for legend says that if the ravens go, the kingdom will fall.

At least six are always on duty, at taxpayers' expense (in fact there are ten: six full-time and four in training). They have their own official, the Ravenmaster, to care for them. Each has one wing clipped to hamper flight, so they truly are prisoners in the Tower.

Charles II's Astronomer Royal complained that the ravens perched on his telescopes and fouled them. He wanted them out, but it was the observatory that got the boot (down the river to Greenwich) and the ravens that stayed.

During the Second World War all but one of the Tower ravens died from the shock of the bombing, but one clung on to save the nation. His name was Grip!

The oldest raven to serve in the Tower was Jim Crow, who died aged 44.

During the 2006 bird flu scare the ravens were kept indoors. Britain was taking no chances!

You'd better believe it!

WITHOUT THE RAVENS
THERE WOULD BE NO
TOWER - AND NO KINGDOM

A NEW KNIGHT WINS HIS SPURS

CHAPTER TWO

KINGS, LORDS AND KNIGHTS

 ife in the castle was run on the assumption that war, if not actually outside the castle gate, was just round the corner. A lord had to have warriors constantly on hand. They didn't all live in the castle, but he could call on them when he needed them. He could count on them turning up to fight for him because they were in his debt: they owed him loyalty because he had given them the land they lived on.

This system – the feudal system – held good right from the top. The king owned all the land and parcelled it out among the great

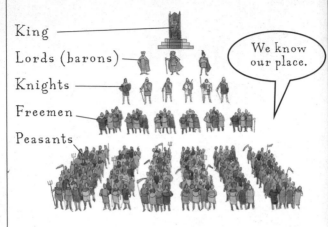

King

Lords (barons)

Knights

Freemen

Peasants

We know our place.

lords, his vassals (dependants), on the strict understanding that, in a crisis, each would provide him with a specified number of mounted warriors, called knights.

The number of knights to be supplied depended on the value of the land granted. Lords shared out their obligation by granting some of their land to lesser nobles, who in turn became their vassals, and so on down the scale. The whole system depended on loyalty, and it worked, partly because of the keen sense of honour there was in those days and partly because people knew which side their bread was buttered on.

FRACTURED KNIGHTS

As time went by, knights reluctant to give up home comforts for castle duty or fighting were allowed to pay money instead. The sum a vassal paid his overlord was still reckoned in knights, and, where property had been split and split again, a smallholder might have to pay $\frac{1}{2}$, or $\frac{1}{4}$, or $\frac{1}{8}$, right down to $\frac{1}{30}$ of a knight.

FRACTIOUS KNIGHTS

In 1198 the abbot of Bury St Edmunds was required to send knights to fight for the king in Normandy. (The clergy held land on similar terms to lay people.) His own men refused to go, on the grounds that their duty didn't oblige them to cross the sea. The abbot had to hire some knights at 3 shillings (15 p) a day.

We'll do it, but it'll cost you.

BECOMING A KNIGHT

Knights were highly skilled mounted warriors trained for the cavalry charge and hand-to-hand fighting. They rode full tilt into battle, jostling for places in the front.

A knight's training began at about the age of seven when he was sent to live in the castle of his father's overlord, or of a relative, to serve as a page.

A page's first lessons were in learning how to behave, in suitably aristocratic fashion, towards his superiors. The rules were strict. At mealtimes he waited on the lord of the castle at table, a duty no hired servant could perform. He had to present his lord's wine cup on bended knee, know the correct handling of the napkin, and master the complicated art of carving meat at the table. Each type of joint required a special approach.

CORRECT TERMS FOR CARVING MEAT

You:

- **break** a deer
- **rear** a goose
- **sauce** a capon
- **spoil** a hen
- **unbrace** a mallard
- **display** a crane
- **disfigure** a peacock
- **allay** a pheasant
- **wing** a partridge
- **thigh** a pigeon.

Pheasant (serving suggestion)

Outdoors, a page learned to ride and groom a horse and to gain basic fighting skills, using a wooden sword.

At around 15 he became squire to a knight and handled real weapons. He looked after his knight's arms and his horse, helped prepare him for battle and followed him into the fight. When he had shown on the battlefield that he was made of the right stuff, he was dubbed a knight.

There was not much ceremony about this in the early days – all that was needed was a blow on the shoulder from someone already a knight. It could be done in the midst of battle. Afterwards, to mark the occasion, the new knight gave a riding display to show his skill in managing horse and armour.

1160   1265   1330   1400   1450

A knight had to be properly fitted out with armour if he were to have any chance of surviving in aggressive hand-to-hand fighting. By the 11th century the leather hauberks used in earlier days had given way to tunics of chain mail (tiny interlinked metal rings). Underneath the mail he wore a *gambeson*, a padded garment that deadened blows and helped to stop arrows biting into flesh. His body was protected by a long shield and his head by a helmet. This was conical at first, with a nose-guard, and later an all-enclosing cake-tin shape that rested on the shoulders.

When a knight charged at the enemy he was prevented from falling off by his high, built-up saddle and his stirrups. He hoped to unhorse his opponent with his lance at the first charge. When it came to close combat he used a sword or a battleaxe.

An axe could cut through chain mail, driving metal links into the wound. Plate armour was the answer to this. It began as small pieces of metal placed at vulnerable points such as elbows and knees. By the 15th century it had developed into entire suits of metal plates.

KITTING OUT A KNIGHT

A knight had to provide his own equipment – and it wasn't cheap.

The most expensive item was his horse. A knight needed a *destrier*, the strongest type of horse, that was bred for carrying the weight of an armoured knight in battle. For everyday use people rode a lighter horse, called a palfrey. A lord would also have swift coursers for hunting.

Armour was also very valuable. It was made to last more than one lifetime. People often mentioned it in wills. For example, Bartholomew de Leigh, a knight who died around 1230, left a hauberk and mailed shoes to the earl of Winchester; he left another small hauberk, with a mail coif (hood), to W. Bordel, while his nephew got a hauberk, mail stockings and a mail covering for a horse. All of this Bartholomew had originally inherited from his brother.

TAKE GOOD CARE OF YOUR ARMOUR

Chain mail needed to be kept clean and polished if it wasn't to be eaten up with rust. It was put in a barrel with sand and vinegar and rolled about vigorously to scour away the rust.

Plate armour was polished by rubbing with bran, or with a pad of that very nasty weed called mare's-tail, which has flint-like particles in its stems.

But too much reliance on armour and stylised training could be disastrous. At the battle of Benevento in 1266 an invading French army was fighting heavily armoured German cavalry. The Germans seemed unbeatable, advancing like metal-clad machines. Then a French soldier noticed that when they raised their swords to strike, their armpits were uncovered. The French closed in tightly, thrust their short daggers upwards and slaughtered the enemy.

Danger area

My suit gives full underarm protection. Does yours?

Don't chance your arm!

THE CASTLE STAFF

There was always a garrison of knights living in the castle, but in peacetime a much larger number would be at home farming their estates. They were available to fight when needed, and they had to do duty as castle guard on a rota basis. The length of duty varied. In the 12th century a knight was expected to serve two months a year in time of war and 40 days' castle guard in peacetime.

When the lord was away, the knights were commanded by the constable of the castle. He became the lord's deputy, responsible for the proper functioning of the entire estate. If the lord had many castles he might appoint constables to be permanently in charge of them.

The constable's right-hand men were the marshal and the estate steward. The marshal was responsible for seeing that the defences were in good order, for the drilling and equipment of the soldiers and for supervising the stables.

Just a few of the household staff

The estate steward managed the lord's business affairs. He worked closely with the bailiffs of the various manors (separate areas of the estate) to make sure the land was yielding enough to keep the castle well fed. He also collected the lord's rents and taxes from the tenants, together with fines for their various wrongdoings – which were a useful additional income for the castle. Offenders were tried at a court that was held regularly in the castle, where the local sheriff or the lord himself sat in judgement.

who made the castle self-sufficient

THE MAN THEY LOVED TO HATE

The bailiff's job was to see that the peasants didn't slack. As a result he was never popular outside the castle. There were plenty of tales told of greedy or dishonest bailiffs. A really mean one is said to have persuaded his lord to sell the sunshine – by charging twelve pennies for every cloth put out to dry in the sun.

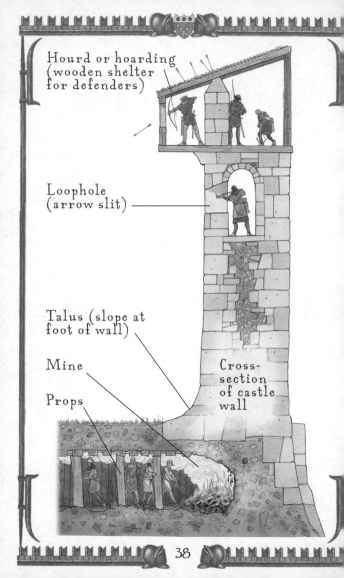

Hourd or hoarding
(wooden shelter
for defenders)

Loophole
(arrow slit)

Talus (slope at
foot of wall)

Mine

Props

Cross-
section
of castle
wall

CHAPTER THREE

SIEGE STORIES

he idea of a siege was to surround your enemy's castle (or camp, or city) so that no-one could get in or out. Then he had to surrender – or starve. It's hardly an exaggeration to say that medieval warfare was 1% battles and 99% sieges. You couldn't take over enemy territory without capturing every castle you met on your way, and unless the gate was opened to you that meant a siege. It was dangerous to ignore one and press on. You would have a hostile garrison behind you which could attack your supply chain, and if you had to retreat its forces were waiting to cut you off.

Setting siege to a castle was a challenge to its owner. If the owner was a king or a great lord, he might not actually be there – he could be at one of his other castles. But if he failed to protect any one of his castles he lost authority. If he could, he sent a 'relieving force' to come at the besiegers from behind and drive them off. It might arrive in time, it might not. That was one of the many things that had to be weighed up in deciding whether to surrender a castle or to abandon a siege. Others were:

• **The time of year**
A lot depended on this because food, or the lack of it, was crucial. In late summer the besiegers could raid the ripening crops and grazing animals in the fields. Later or earlier in the year they would be much more dependent on supplies arriving from home. Autumn favoured the castle, when it would be well stocked with harvested crops and meat salted for winter.

• **Advance warning**
Had there been time to lay waste all the surrounding land, leaving nothing to support the besiegers (or the unlucky local peasants)?

• **Who will starve first**

It wasn't always the castle that gave up through starvation, though there are many horror stories of people eating boiled boots and dead bodies. A big besieging army might run out of food quicker than a well-stocked castle (or their men might get demoralised and desert – an option not open to the castle dwellers).

• **Water**

Did the castle have a reliable water supply? Could the besiegers cut it off at source, or poison it?

• **The weather**

A scorching summer could dry up the castle's well. But it could also help spread diseases like dysentery in the besiegers' camp. It's recorded that at Le Sap in Normandy in the 12th century, the attackers – who had meat but nothing else – ate it raw (not a good idea in warm weather) and got appalling diarrhoea. They were forced to abandon the siege, 'by God's judgement', and 'left a trail of filth behind, many barely capable of dragging themselves back home'.

SIEGE WEAPONS

Once attackers got inside the bailey, a siege was more than half won. Getting past the bailey walls was the big problem. Basically you had to get over, under or through them.

OVER

The obvious way to scale a wall is by ladder, but walls were often too high for them and they were only safe in a surprise attack. Otherwise they could be toppled back by defenders waiting on the battlements. It was more effective to use a 'belfry' or siege tower. This movable wooden tower, several storeys high, was wheeled up to the walls (the moat had to be filled in with brushwood first) and delivered a large number of armed men, all at once, to the top of the wall. The belfry's sides and roof had to be covered with wet ox-hides because the defenders would do everything they could to set it alight. Once on fire, the belfry was a death-trap.

Drawbridge

Belfry

Wet hides

Moat

Brushwood

For getting missiles over there was plenty of choice. Both sides relied heavily on archery. By the 12th century the 'pull back the string and let it twang' bow was old technology. The new thing was the crossbow – so lethal that the Church banned it when it first appeared. Its string was drawn back by putting one's foot in a sort of stirrup to hold the bow down and then yanking with both hands. It delivered a metal bolt at a speed that sent it right through armour.

For attackers its disadvantage was its rate of fire. It took a long time to load, making firers standing targets (until special shields were developed). But for defenders hiding behind battlements it was the weapon of choice.

Crossbowmen with a pavise (movable shield)

Mangonel

Siege engines – machinery for hurling missiles – went back to Roman times. There was the mangonel, with a throwing arm that was winched back and released, and the ballista, which worked like a giant crossbow.

Ballista

In the 12th century the Arabs devised a more powerful machine, the trebuchet. It worked like an unbalanced see-saw. A rock or a big ball of lead was put in a sling hanging from the longer arm, and a huge counterweight (such as a crate filled with up to two tonnes of earth) was heaved up and held aloft on the shorter arm. Four or five men hauling on ropes could do this in about five minutes. When they let go, the short arm crashed down, flipping the missile up and over.

Trebuchet

45

Trebuchets could fling all sorts of things: pots of Greek fire (see page 57), heads, animals, dung. At Auberoche in 1345 a page bringing a message from the English in the castle was sent back via trebuchet, with the message tied round his neck.

A particularly clever defenders' up-and-over device was the crow, a sort of giant fishing rod with a claw on the end, designed to scoop up good hostage material. In 1139 Prince Henry of Scotland narrowly escaped being hooked at the siege of Ludlow. He was dragged from his horse but managed to escape.

PERSONALISED

Military commanders were fond of their siege machines and gave them nicknames.

Edward I of England had trebuchets called Vicar, Parson, Robynet, Forster and Warwolf.

Richard Cœur de Lion called the giant belfry he used at the siege of Acre Mategriffon (Checkmate).

THROUGH

Knocking your way through thick stone walls was no pushover but powerful trebuchets would do the job, given time. You grouped them together and hurled rocks at a section of wall till it crumbled. At Rouen in 1174 men worked the trebuchets in 8-hour shifts to keep the attack going night and day.

You might break though quicker using a batterering ram, also known as a 'cat'. This was a heavy length of wood with a metal tip. It was slung horizontally in a frame and swung back and forth against the base of the wall. It had to be well protected since people on the walls were sure to drop stones and pots of fire on it.

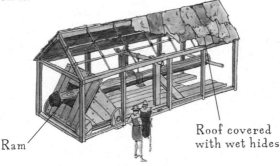

Ram

Roof covered
with wet hides

UNDER

Mining (see page 38) was the most feared form of attack because it was hard to detect – provided the mine's starting point was some way away and well hidden. The miners dug a tunnel, shored up with wooden props, till they got under the foundations of the wall. Then they set fire to the props. The tunnel roof collapsed and brought down the wall.

That's how the great square keep at Rochester Castle fell to King John in 1215. 'Send to us with all speed', he commanded, 'forty of the fattest pigs to bring fire beneath the tower.' In the days before gunpowder you needed something to get a big fire going. The pigs were rendered down for fat which was poured into barrels and rolled into the mine.

With a corner of the keep gone, Rochester's starving defenders fought on, saving food by the classic siege strategy of ejecting everyone too old, ill or weak (i.e. female) to fight. No mercy was shown to such people, stranded between the shut castle gate and the enemy. King John had their hands and feet cut off.

SOME SIEGE DEATHS – AND A NEAR THING

At the siege of Antioch (1097–1098) a Turk killed by Godfrey of Bouillon was riding so fast he was sliced in half 'like a young leek'. His upper half fell to the ground and his lower half rode on into the city.

At Caen, in 1417, a knight called Sir Edward Springhouse fell off a scaling ladder into the ditch below. The French dropped burning straw on him and roasted him in his armour.

Simon de Montfort (French father of Simon de Montfort the English baron) was killed at the siege of Toulouse in 1218 by a mangonel powered by 'women, ladies and young girls'. They hit him with a stone that cracked his head open. Good shot, girls.

At Acre, during the Crusades, a knight squatting down to relieve himself was attacked from behind with a lance. ('How base', said the person reporting it, 'to take a knight thus unawares.') He managed to jump aside, grab a stone, bash his attacker on the head with it (fatally) and capture his horse.

SIEGE CHIVALRY

There were certain rules (often forgotten) in conducting sieges.

• The head of the besieging force must first send in a formal demand for surrender. If it was rejected, the besiegers threw a missile at the castle gate as a sign that the siege was officially under way. Anyone attempting to pass through the gate after that was liable to be killed.

• A knight who surrendered was under the protection of his captor and should be allowed to lead a normal life, within obvious limits. This part of the code often slipped people's minds. An unfortunate knight called Henry Gentian was not only locked up in a cell with snakes but had his teeth bashed in with a hammer to make him agree to a larger ransom.

• If one gave one's word one must stick to it – another rule frequently overlooked, though nobly honoured by Talbot, Earl of Shrewsbury, in the 15th century. He was captured by the French and promised never to bear arms against them. Later he led an English attack, on horseback but without armour. Of course, he was killed.

• A monarch's person was sacred. When an archer aimed his crossbow at King John during the siege of Rochester, another defender stopped him firing, on the grounds that a mere man should not end the life of a king. It was for God to deal with kings.

🏰 FLIGHT OF FANCY

A sheriff of Essex, in the time of Henry III, proposed taking 40 cockerels, tying fire-bombs to them and flying them over the enemy's walls. Fortunately peace was made in time, and if the cockerels did get cooked it was not until later.

Yikes!

THE DIRTY TRICKS DEPARTMENT

• Try some torture

When Norman baron William of Breteuil was captured during the siege of his castle at Ivry he was tortured, kept in a dungeon for three months and then made to stand in a wet shirt, on a high place, in a cold wind, until he agreed to hand over the castle.

• Give your opponent a nasty turn

When Emperor Frederick Barbarossa set siege to the Italian city of Crema in 1159, he let his men cut off the heads of captives and play football with them. In reply the citizens tore their captives limb from limb on the city walls. The tit for tat continued. When Frederick's siege engines got a battering from the city, he ordered hostages, including children, to be tied to the fronts of them. The city preferred firing at its children to surrendering. Commentators saw no wrong in the emperor's actions – he was fighting a 'just war' – but the citizens were blamed for their 'barbarity'. (They had to surrender in the end.)

• **Throwing decaying animals** (or even humans) into a city to spread infection was an old trick. The Turks at the siege of Rhodes in 1522 improved on the idea. They studded the carcasses with sharp bits of metal so that when they hit someone the wound became septic.

• **Get the defenders excommunicated**
It lowers the men's morale. They'll be less willing to die fighting if they think they're going straight to hell. This was Henry III's ploy at the siege of Bedford Castle in 1224.

• **Think outside the box**
The attackers of the Rhineland fortress of Husterknupp sent a message to the lady of the castle that she could leave before things got really bad, and take out whatever she could carry. She came out of the castle gate with her husband on her back.

• **It was beneath one's honour** to use really low-class tricks. A chronicler of the Fourth Crusade was disgusted when the keys of a stronghold were obtained by getting its constable drunk in a tavern: 'It was not fitting for a noble lord even to have thought of it.'

CHAPTER four

CRUSADER CASTLES

Jerusalem, a holy city for Christians, Muslims and Jews, had been in Muslim hands since the 7th century. On the whole, its Arab rulers had been prepared to tolerate the flood of Christians who regularly made pilgrimages there. Then in the 11th century new conquerors swept into Jerusalem – the warlike Seljuk Turks, a much less easy-going lot. They stopped the pilgrims coming. It was in response to this that Pope Urban II, in 1095, called upon all Christians everywhere to free Jerusalem from the Turks.

Thousands responded to the Pope's call and set off for the Holy Land. An army made up mostly of French and Norman knights (collectively known as Franks) gathered together at Constantinople. It made a long, hard march through Anatolia (modern Turkey), captured the city of Antioch after a savage siege, and by July 1099 was outside the walls of Jerusalem. The journey had taken four years.

Jerusalem fell after a horrific siege which lasted a month. During that time the Franks sat outside the city walls, very much reduced in numbers, with their tents rotten and with almost no food or water. The Muslims, much better off, drove them away again and again, toppling their scaling ladders and pelting them with stones, arrows and containers of a terrible substance called Greek fire that burst into flames on impact.

GREEK FIRE

No-one knows for sure who invented Greek fire or what was in it. The Byzantines were using it in the 7th century AD, but the recipe was a well-kept secret. They claimed it had been revealed by an angel to their first Christian emperor, Constantine, and that an official about to betray its formula had been struck down in flames on the steps of the cathedral of Santa Sofia.

Many attempts were made to guess what was in it. One recipe suggested live sulphur, tartar (an acid), sarcocolla (a vegetable gum) and pitch, boiled salt and petroleum. Others included the bile of a tortoise, dolphin fat, luminous worms and the tail of a green lizard.

Don't forget the eye of newt and toe of frog.

My gran used to put chilli in it.

The Franks worked non-stop to build belfries. It was time-consuming because timber was scarce and had to be brought long distances. Filling the city's moat with stones and rubbish to get the belfries to the walls took three days and nights. Then, hurling burning sacks and cushions over the walls as a smoke screen, the Franks were over and into the city at last.

A hideous massacre of its citizens followed. That was to be expected according to the rules of siege war, but the extreme ferocity of the Crusaders was noted at the time. It was said that they waded in blood up to their ankles.

Jerusalem, as imagined by a European
artist of the 15th century

The Franks shared out the land they'd gained
– a long strip along the Syrian and Palestinian
coast – to form four Crusader States. Then
they had to face the problem of holding on to
them. Their solution was the traditional
Norman one: to build castles at strategic
points, from which their knights rode out and
forced the locals into submitting to the same
system of overlordship, payments and rough
justice as they did at home.

This first success gave the Crusaders confidence. They thrust their castles eastward into Muslim territory, choosing sites with natural protection, such as a steep-sided spur of rock. Such places had usually already been fortified for thousands of years. The Franks seized them and rebuilt.

The great Crusader castles of Saone, Beaufort and Krak des Chevaliers show how ingenious they were at strengthening a site. At Saone, clamped on a mountain spur, they isolated the castle by cutting away around 120,000 tonnes of solid rock to make an artificial gorge over 20 metres wide. They left a single needle of stone, 30 metres high, standing in the middle of the gorge to carry a bridge. It is still there to see.

Many Frankish knights thought they had a better chance of a good life in the conquered Holy Land than if they went home. Very much outnumbered by resentful Muslims, they made some attempt to meet them halfway by adapting to local ways, as far as their Christian consciences allowed. This was no great hardship, as in arts, sciences and social manners the Muslims were their superiors.

Usamah Ibn-Munqidh, Lord of Shaizar, who was a poet as well as a warrior, had mixed feelings about the Franks. 'Allah,' he wrote, 'saw them as possessing the virtues of courage and fighting, but nothing else.' He did not think much of their medical skill. A local doctor treating a Crusader's abscessed leg with poultices was thrust aide by a Frankish physician who asked the man whether he wanted to die with two legs or live with one. He chose living with one, so a knight was told to chop his leg off with an axe. The marrow spurted out and he died at once.

Usamah admitted that Franks who had lived longer in the East were better than recent comers, but he said they were the exception.

GOING NATIVE

Sterner Christians deplored the Eastern ways of the lax Franks:

- walking in long, wide-sleeved silk vestments, trimmed with gold and studded with pearls

- wearing the *keffiyeh* (Arab headdress)

- growing a Muslim-style beard

- veiling their wives

- hiring professional mourners at funerals

- listening to strange-sounding Arab music

- visiting dancing girls.

Who cares? Bring on the dancing girls.

What would the folks back home say?

62

Frankish rulers adopted an Eastern court style, appointed eunuchs as court officials and had suppliants approach on bended knee. The Frankish King of Jerusalem sat cross-legged to give audiences, dressed in a gold-embroidered burnous (Arab cloak). Tancred, Frankish regent of Antioch, wore a turban, though for the sake of appearances he pinned a cross on it.

There was a certain amount of understanding between Eastern and Western leaders. Princely hostages were frequently well treated; joint hunting parties were sometimes arranged, the Franks learning how to use cheetahs to hunt gazelle.

When the great Muslim commander Saladin was besieging the castle of Karak, it happened that the wedding of its heir was taking place inside. Meat and wine from the feast were sent out to the Muslim forces and Saladin courteously asked which tower the bridal pair were sleeping in, so he could avoid bombarding it.

A TOUCH OF EASTERN SPLENDOUR

Thirteenth-century Crusader Wildebrand of Oldenburg describes Arab sophistication in a Frankish castle in Beirut:

The floor of the chamber is paved with mosaic representing water ruffled by a light breeze, and as one walks one is surprised that one's footsteps leave no trace on the sand that is represented below.

The walls of the room are covered with strips of marble which form a panelling of great beauty. The vaulted roof is painted to look like the sky. In the middle of the room is a fountain in marbles of various colours, wonderfully polished. A dragon in the fountain appears to devour a number of animals.

A limpid and gushing jet of water, together with the air that wafts through the open windows, lends the room a delicious freshness.

The Crusades of following centuries all petered out in varying degrees of disaster. From the 12th century onward the far-outnumbered Franks were increasingly under Muslim attack. Despite recruits from Europe their numbers and revenues shrank. Many were ruined by having to pay enormous ransoms and by the cost of maintaining castles and men at arms. They sold or gave away their castles and withdrew to a pleasanter life in the coastal cities. Luckily for them, there were some aggressively warlike Christians who were more than willing to take the castles on. These were the orders of fighting monks, the Hospitallers and Templars.

The Knights Hospitallers had begun as volunteers, looking after pilgrims to the Holy Land in the mid-11th century, finding them places to stay and caring for the sick. But in 1113 the Pope recognised them as a religious order of fighting monks. They took monastic vows but were dedicated warriors.

The Knights Templar, taking their name from King Solomon's temple at Jerusalem, and the Teutonic Knights who fought the heathen Slavs of north-eastern Europe, were similar military orders. The orders were fanatical spreaders and defenders of Christianity. Gifts of property from pious people all over Europe made them rich, and their vows of chastity, poverty and obedience made them ideal candidates for life on the desert fringe.

MEET A HOSPITALLER

'They never dress gaily, and wash but seldom. Shaggy by reason of their uncombed hair, they are begrimed with dust, and swarthy from the weight of their armour and the heat of the sun.

They do their utmost to possess strong and swift horses, but their mounts are not garnished with ornaments nor decked with trappings, for they think of battle and victory, not of pomp and show. Such has God chosen for his own.'

This is St Bernard of Clairvaux, inspirer of the Second Crusade, speaking. You can see that a Hospitaller would make no attempt to copy Muslim ways or reach a compromise with them.

Yes, it's a man's life in the Knights Hospitallers.

The greatest Crusader castle of all, Krak des Chevaliers in Syria, was largely a creation of the Hospitallers. It stands in a commanding position on an abrupt spur of hill that dominates the Syrian plain. This important site already had a small Arab fort on it when the Crusaders swept past on their way to Jerusalem in 1099. Eleven years later they replaced it with a big new castle.

By 1142, running the castle was proving too much for its owner, the Count of Tripoli, who gave it to the Hospitallers. They expanded

Krak des Chevaliers is still largely intact today.

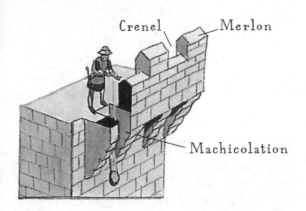

Crenel · Merlon · Machicolation

it into the largest Crusader fortress in the Holy Land. They gave it an additional circle of walls, 3 metres thick, with seven guard towers. This was a big advance in the science of fortification, producing a 'concentric' castle with two strong lines of defence, one within the other. They used machicolations (overhanging parapets from which missiles were dropped through holes in the floor), portcullises and hairpin entrances. The walls were given enormous taluses (sheer sloping masses of masonry against their lower parts). This made them almost impossible to scale or undermine, and the sloping surface made dropped missiles ricochet unpredictably onto attackers.

The castle could house 50 to 60 Hospitallers and up to 2,000 foot soldiers. Its vast underground storage chambers held enough grain to feed a garrison for years. It had ample stabling, dovecotes, and – the latest Eastern technology – a windmill on the battlements.

At least twelve times the Muslims besieged Krak and failed to take it. Saladin took a look at it and withdrew without trying. An Arab writer described it as sticking like a bone in Muslim throats.

It was taken at last by the Mamluk Sultan Baibars, in 1271, not by pounding from his enormous trebuchets, but through a trick. He presented a forged letter from the Crusader Commander in Tripoli, ordering the defenders to surrender. Otherwise, this immensely strong castle would probably never have fallen.

Twenty years later, with the destruction of the port of Acre, the Crusaders lost their last stronghold in the Holy Land. Two centuries of crusading had ended in complete failure.

AT HOME IN A CASTLE

 he lord and his knights, and all those workers out in the bailey, expected a square meal on the table when they needed it. It was the job of the lord's wife, the lady of the castle, to see that this, and every other part of the castle's domestic routine, ran smoothly.

She didn't do the work herself, of course. but she had to make sure it was being done properly.

HOW THE LADY OF THE CASTLE SHOULD BEHAVE

From a book of manners written by a retired Crusader, 1265:

She should:

- be obedient and chaste

- look straight ahead, with a tranquil air, not too high and not too low

- walk erect, with dignity, neither trotting nor running

- avoid anger and high words

- be careful not to eye men as the sparrowhawk does the lark

- not bestow lavish gifts on people. (That is her husband's privilege. The only gifts a woman should make are to the poor – provided she has her husband's permission.)

The lady's right-hand man was the house steward. He had a most responsible job, for as well as superintending the work of the castle's many servants he had to ensure that its cellars were always well stocked with food, drink and all the other necessary things like oil (for lamps), wax (for candles), salt, honey and spices. If he got it wrong there were no shops to run out to. He had to think in terms of a year, from harvest to harvest. For precious things like spices and sugar he had to wait for the great annual trade fair.

The steward (left) worked alongside the chamberlain, who saw that everything was properly provided in the hall and chambers.

FEEDING THE CASTLE

The catering staff was made up of the pantler, head of the pantry where the bread was stored; the butler (bottler), who looked after drink in the buttery (the place where barrels, or 'butts', were kept); and the cook and his scullions (kitchen assistants), who worked in the separate kitchen in the bailey. They roasted the meat over the fire, on a spit turned by hand, or simmered it in a great round-bottomed cauldron.

Butler

GARBAGE

Here's a 14th-century recipe from the master cook of King Richard II of England:

Take good giblets (garbage), chickens' heads, feet, livers and gizzards, and wash them clean. Throw them into a nice pot, and add fresh beef broth, powdered pepper, cinnamon, cloves, mace, parsley and sage chopped small.

Then take bread, steep it in the same broth, draw it through a strainer, add and let boil till done. Add powdered ginger, verjuice (sour grape juice), salt and a little saffron, and serve.

Cook and scullions

There were usually two meals a day, the main one a formal dinner at about the fifth hour of daylight. (The actual time, by our reckoning, varied with the seasons. The medieval working day, which was from sunrise to sunset, was divided into twelve equal hours, so medieval hours were longer in summer than in winter.)

The hall in the keep was for ceremonial dining. Normally everyone in the castle had meals together in a large wooden hall in the bailey. The lord and his family ate on a raised platform across the end of the hall. Everyone else sat, in order of rank, at trestle tables along the length of it. You brought your own knife to the table and usually shared a drinking cup. Several cooked dishes were put on the table at the same time and you dolloped your helping onto the trencher (slice of stale bread) that was placed on your wooden platter to mop up the juices.

MIND YOUR MANNERS

Books of table manners warned you not to:

- wipe your knife on the tablecloth
- dip your meat in the salt cellar
- put your thumb in the drinking cup.

Dining in the keep of Hedingham
Castle, Essex, England

The usual drink was the castle's home-brewed ale. Wine was enjoyed when it was new, but it didn't keep. By summer it was sour or mouldy, and sometimes so muddy that people had to strain it through their teeth before swallowing. But even this was better than drinking water, which was well known to make you ill (because it was full of bacteria).

Fish was the only flesh that could be eaten in Lent. In England, fresh Yarmouth herrings were a great delicacy (delicious flavoured with ginger, pepper and cinnamon and made into a pie). But, apart from occasional treats from the lord's fishponds, people living inland could only eat salted fish. By the end of Lent they were heartily sick of it.

The Countess of Leicester's household, in the 13th century, ate up to a thousand herrings a day during Lent.

LENTEN COMPLAINT

A 15th-century schoolboy laments:

Thou wilt not believe how weary I am of fish, and how much I desire that flesh were come again, for I have ate none other but salt fish this Lent, and it hath engendered so much phlegm within me that it stoppeth my pipes and I can barely speak or breathe.

For cod's sake! I've haddock up to here.

Furniture was limited to beds, tables (normally consisting just of boards placed on trestles) and a few chairs, or more often benches. Walls were whitewashed or brightly painted, and hard chairs and window seats were softened with cushions, thick woollen fabrics and furs.

Clothes, hangings and valuables were kept in chests, bound with iron and closed with lock and key. These were kept in good order by the keeper of the wardrobe – an important storage room where not only clothes but anything of value – gold or silver plate, jewellery, expensive spices – was locked up out of harm's way.

Jangle!

HOUSEHOLD TIPS

- Bedding feathers must never be washed but shaken and aired in the bread oven.

- Chew the baby's meat before you give it, to prevent choking.

- Birch twigs at the bottom of the stew pot will stop meat from catching.

- Goose feathers are good for arrows but no use for stuffing mattresses. For those you need the feathers of a bird that swims.

- Mullein leaves keep away cockroaches.

- Ash is the best timber for the fire. Elm and alder are the worst. Resinous woods are little use; they give off sparks and black smoke.

- To launder sheets: steep them in wood ash and urine.

- Hang venison round the smoke-hole in the kitchen roof. It's the only fly-proof spot.

The most important piece of furniture was the lord and lady's great bed in their chamber. It had a feather mattress and fur-lined coverlets and was enclosed at night by linen hangings suspended from poles, to give warmth and privacy.

The ladies in waiting slept on truckle beds in the chamber. Even these were a luxury. Most people had a straw pallet thrown onto a bench in the hall or directly on the floor. The dried rushes that covered the floor were given a new layer when they got grubby. Four times a year the whole lot was changed, by which time it must have been quite a layer-cake of spillages and droppings.

FIVE TOP TIPS FOR FIGHTING FLEAS

- Scour the floor with wormwood.
- Strew the room with alder leaves.
- Catch them on bread trenchers slimed with glue.
- Put rough cloth or sheepskin on the bed or about the room. The fleas will get stuck in it.
- Fold clothes very tightly and shut them in chests. The fleas will die from lack of light and air.

FIVE GOOD WAYS OF WAGING WAR ON FLIES

- Hang up strings soaked in honey for them to stick to.
- Put down a bowl of milk and hare's gall. They will settle on it and be poisoned.
- Tie sprigs of fern in little tassels and hang them up. Flies will gather on them in the evening. Take the sprigs down and throw them away.
- The juice of red onion will kill them.
- Flies will not bother a horse that has been rubbed with butter or old salty grease.

KEEPING CLEAN

People washed their hands before eating, and at the end of a meal water was brought to the table for washing greasy fingers.

All-over washing was more of a problem, but higher-ranking people took a bath from time to time. A servant brought a wooden tub to their chamber. It was rather like a half-barrel and was lined with cloth in case of splinters. Some had a hanging canopy to keep off draughts. Even so, the water must soon have got cold.

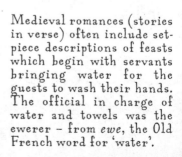

Medieval romances (stories in verse) often include set-piece descriptions of feasts which begin with servants bringing water for the guests to wash their hands. The official in charge of water and towels was the ewerer – from *ewe*, the Old French word for 'water'.

THE LADY OF THE CASTLE ENJOYS SOME 'ME TIME'

Advice to a Trainee Servant
c. 1460

- Do not claw your head or your back as if you were after a flea, or stroke your hair as if you sought a louse.

- Be not glum; and keep your eyes from winking and wavering.

- Do not pick your nose or let it drop clear pearls, or blow it too hard, lest your lord hear.

- Twist not your neck askew like a jackdaw; wring not your hands with picking or trifling or shrugging, as if you would saw wood; nor puff up your chest, nor pick your ears.

- Do not lick a dish with your tongue to get out dust.

- Good son, do not pick your teeth, or grind or gnash them, or with puffing and blowing cast foul breath upon your lord.

NOW FOR THE BASICS

Lavatories, and sometimes urinals (small triangular openings in the wall), were provided in the keep, usually built into the thickness of the outside wall of a chamber.

In 1246 King Henry III wrote to his constable at the Tower:

Since the privy chamber [lavatory] in our wardrobe at London is in an undue and improper place, wherefore it smells badly, we command you that you in no wise omit to cause another privy chamber to be made in such more fitting and proper place as you may select there, even though it should cost a hundred pounds.

A huge sum for the smallest room!

Lavatories were wooden seats with a hole in them that let everything drop down a chute and through an outside opening at the bottom of the wall. Then it went into the moat, if there was one. Otherwise it piled up at the base of the wall, or in a cesspit, until it was carted off by specialist operators called 'dung farmers'.

WHAT'S IN A NAME?

The 1375 accounts for Queenborough Castle record that payment for cleaning out the castle cesspit was made to professional pit-clearers William Mokking and Nicholas Richandgood.

Dung farmers must have adjusted well to working conditions, for one of them is said to have complained, outside working hours, of the smell of a badly snuffed candle.

Privy chamber*

*Garderobe was another favoured euphemism.

To moat

CHAPTER SIX

THE CASTLE IMPROVED

he square stone keeps of Norman times were a big advance on wooden ones. Their walls were stronger, they didn't catch fire and they could be built much taller. However, before long their drawbacks began to show.

AWKWARD ANGLES

Unpleasant experiences like the one at Rochester (see page 48), where miners brought down a whole corner of the keep, showed that corners were a weak point. They could be undermined. And there was another problem with corners: when archers peered through the arrow-slits they only had a good view of the land directly in front of them. What lay to their far left and right was blocked by the wall they were looking from. There was always a blind spot at the angle of the keep where enemies could lurk unseen.

So corners had to go!

In the 12th century various new forms of keep were tried: octagonal keeps, and round keeps with projecting turrets. Henry II of England was a great experimenter. It's said he never went anywhere without his copy of Vegetius, a treatise on fortification written by an ancient Roman that was much studied in the 12th and 13th centuries.

Henry tried a polygonal keep at Orford Castle, Suffolk, in 1165. He gave it so many small sides that it is almost circular, and added three flanking towers. A flanking tower was one that stuck forward from a wall, so that defenders could fire sideways along the wall. Vegetius had hotly recommended them.

If they were set close enough, attackers nearing the wall could be shot at from towers on either side of them.

A rounded keep avoided blind spots, but if you added flanking towers you partly blocked the archers' view. The answer to this was to put the towers in the bailey walls, which then took over from the keep as a castle's main line of defence.

At Dover Castle in Kent, Henry tried a square keep surrounded by a double ring of walls, each with flanking towers. On the outer ring, finished by his son John, the tower walls were curved. Though these ideas were around in the East at the time (they were used by the Hospitallers at Krak des Chevaliers), Dover, begun in 1179, is the earliest 'concentric' castle in Europe.

DOING A MOONLIGHT FLIT

Henry II understood that castles were power, and that too much power in the hands of the barons was not a good thing. His predecessor Stephen, a nice man but weak, had let barons fortify castles and defy him. Many of them thought they'd be better off with his cousin Matilda on the throne. This led to civil war and sieges up and down the country.

At one point, in 1142, Matilda was besieged by Stephen at Oxford castle. After three months the garrison was starving and she'd had enough. It was winter and the countryside was blanketed with snow. Matilda dressed herself in a white sheet as camouflage and was lowered from the walls on a rope. She crossed the frozen moat, slipped past Stephen's pickets and fled across the meadows to supporters at nearby Wallingford.

LUCKILY FOR **M**ATILDA **I**T WAS ALL WHITE ON THE NIGHT

A great spur to castle building at the end of the 12th century was the long-standing rivalry between the kings of France and England. At that time England held lots of land in France and the French king Philip Augustus meant to put a stop to that. Everything came to a head when Richard I of England (Cœur de Lion – Lionheart) built an enormously strong castle on a spur of rock overlooking the river Seine, just where it would block the French from reaching Rouen, his capital in Normandy.

Richard called his new castle Château Gaillard, which means something like 'jaunty castle'. He was certainly laughing in Philip Augustus's face. The French king said he would take it though its walls were made of iron. Richard retorted that he would hold it though its walls were made of butter. He didn't have a chance to prove it, for he was killed by a crossbow bolt two years later, in 1199.

His brother King John rubbed Philip Augustus up the wrong way and gave him a perfect excuse for attacking the castle.

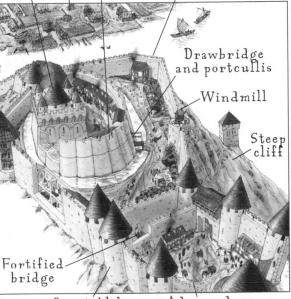

Village
(Les Andelys)

Keep
(donjon)

Inner wall of
novel design

Outer
curtain wall

Drawbridge
and portcullis

Windmill

Steep
cliff

Fortified
bridge

Constable's
tower

Advanced
bastion

CHÂTEAU GAILLARD

It seemed an impossible nut to crack. Richard had used all the defence techniques he'd seen in the East as a Crusader. He'd chosen a site that was protected on three sides by sheer chalk cliffs, and on the fourth he'd had a ditch hewn in the rock. The keep was set in a double ring of walls with the latest round towers. For added protection the main castle was fronted by an advanced bastion – effectively a smaller castle in front of the main one – separated from it by another ditch. The only approach was from this side, so attackers had to capture an outer, then a middle, then an inner courtyard to get to the keep.

Philip Augustus tried in vain to starve the castle into surrender. After his troops had sat outside for six months, he had to act. He gained the outer bailey by mining the wall, but his miners could get no purchase on the sheer walls of the main fortress, even though they tried sticking daggers into the chalk to make themselves a ladder.

Then one of Philip's soldiers came up with a dodge that must be rated number one in the dirty tricks department: he climbed up a lavatory chute. He'd noticed, looking up, that high above the loo outlet was a chapel window, large enough to climb through. He crawled up the chute, got into the chapel and let a party of men in through the window. They raised a great din to make it seem they were a huge force; the defenders panicked and fled to the inner bailey.

The French began mining the inner bailey under the shelter of its connecting bridge. The defenders started a countermine and the two sides between them brought the wall down. The English forces thought it better to come to terms than to make a last stand in the keep, and so Richard's great castle was taken.

Mine and countermine

⚔ CASTLE DRAMA

Marion de la Bruyère was a girl of noble family being brought up in the household of Josse de Dinan, lord of Ludlow Castle in the border country between England and Wales.

In 1160 the castle was besieged by the Lacys, who claimed it was theirs, and a battle was fought before its walls. A page, watching from above, saw Josse overcome by four knights. He seized an axe and rushed out to help, killing two of the knights, capturing the other two and saving the day. Josse proclaimed him a hero and promised to marry him to his daughter.

The captive knights were held in the castle, where one of them, Arnold de Lisle, caught Marion's eye. She fell madly in love with him. He got her to provide him with a knotted rope by which he escaped.

It seems that Marion wasn't suspected. The wedding of Josse's daughter took place and Josse accompanied the bridal couple on their journey from Ludlow.

Marion, aflame with love, sent Arnold a message that the family were away and that she'd let him in by a rope ladder from the same window that he'd escaped by. He went to her room and made love to her, but she did not know that he had left the ladder hanging and that the hundred soldiers he'd brought with him were now in the castle. They killed the watchman and slaughtered the sleeping garrison.

Marion heard screams and realised what her lover had done. She leapt from her bed, seized his sword and ran him through the body, then threw herself from the window to her death on the rocks below.

Josse returned to besiege his own castle, but unsuccessfully. The Lacys kept Ludlow.

Goodbye, cruel world!

A huge amount of money and planning went into the making of a castle. Detailed accounts survive from Edward I's great castle-building programme at Conwy, Harlech and Caernarfon, castles begun in 1283 to keep down the Welsh. Many raw materials – iron, steel, best-quality stone for fireplaces and chimney breasts, lead for roofs and plumbing – were brought from far away at huge cost.

There was a workforce of thousands. Skilled workers included quarriers, stonemasons, blacksmiths, carpenters, plumbers (lead workers) and glaziers. Unskilled labourers did the trenching, shifting and heaving. Some must have been forced into it, for payments were made to three sergeants for escorting 300 diggers 'in case they should flee while on the road'.

The most highly valued craftsmen were the freemasons (so called because they carved the expensive 'freestone' that was fine-grained and could be cut in all directions). They often worked in teams, travelling from one project to the next. The entire building project was supervised by a master mason, a highly skilled person who controlled all the practical aspects of building a castle and might have a big say in its design as well.

A really good master mason was the medieval equivalent of an architect and engineer rolled into one, except that he had been trained the hard way: on building sites, not at college.

Edward I's master mason, Master James of St Georges, had spent many years designing castles for the Count of Savoy before he came to England to mastermind Edward's massive Welsh fortresses. Edward was so pleased with him that he gave him a pension for life and made him constable of Harlech Castle.

Masons

HERE COMES A CHOPPER

Not all great castle-designers were as well rewarded as Master James, according to a 12th-century story about the castle of Ivry, built for Alberede, wife of the Count of Bayeaux.

It was designed by Lanfred, the greatest master mason in France at the time. Alberede was so delighted with it that she had Lanfred beheaded so that he could not build its equal for anyone else.

She sounds horrible, so you might like to know that her husband put her to death – though not for that.

CHAPTER SEVEN

CASTLE ENTERTAINMENTS

 **B**arons and knights were trained for an active life, and when they wanted to enjoy themselves they went outdoors. Hunting and tournaments were their favourite pastimes. A lord would take a hunting party for a whole day in the forest, with servants bringing a picnic. He would be after deer or wild boar. Small animals like hare or rabbits were beneath his attention.

Only kings and people of rank (including members of the Church) could hunt. This was the result of a most unpopular idea called 'forest law' that was brought to England by William the Conqueror. To ensure that he always had the pick of the hunting, William declared huge swathes of land to be royal game reserves.

Later kings kept adding to these 'royal forests'. Anything in them that might upset the game was removed or forbidden. Villages were destroyed, farming banned, no-one could fell trees, and sometimes locals could not even gather firewood or acorns. Poachers could be hanged or mutilated. William II had people blinded merely for disturbing the deer.

This was a change from more easy-going Saxon times, and was much resented by ordinary people who had relied on the forest for food and fuel. Robin Hood and his Sherwood outlaws, whoever they may have been, became folk-heroes in legend for defying the forest law.

If you were in favour with the king, he would grant you a licence to hunt in any part of the royal forest that lay within your land. Then you could make your own regulations and pocket the poaching fines. If you didn't have this privilege, you could stock a stretch of open land with deer to form a hunting park. This didn't need a licence, but if your deer fled into the royal forest and you followed them, you would be punished.

The most aristocratic form of hunting was falconry, in which trained birds of prey swooped down on birds in flight and brought them to the ground. Launching your bird beyond arrow-range to make a strike was a dizzying thrill in the days before guns.

The falcons were looked after by an official called the fowler. Each bird responded to its individual trainer, so nobles usually kept their favourite bird with them: on their wrist, behind their seat at meals, and on a perch in their chamber at night.

CHOOSING A FOWLER

12th-century advice on choosing a fowler:

Look for someone 'sober, alert and sweet of breath.' Avoid 'those from whom the hawks might become infested with vermin.' (An interesting variation on catching a flea from one's pet.)

In medieval falconry the term 'falcon' meant a trained female peregrine falcon, the noblest of all hunting birds. The male peregrine, smaller and less aggressive, was called a 'tiercel'.

No-one was allowed a bird that was above their rank. Only princes and the highest nobles could have a peregrine. A knight could have a saker, his lady a merlin, a squire a lanner and a yeoman a goshawk. A sporting priest was allowed nothing better than a sparrowhawk.

Some falcons were so highly prized that they were literally worth more than their weight in gold. When Sultan Beyazid captured the son of the duke of Normandy, during the Crusades, he turned down the duke's ransom offer of 200,000 gold ducats. Beyazid wanted something worth even more: the duke's twelve white gyrfalcons. He got them.

MAKING TROTTERS TROT

The rules of a certain monastery forbade its monks to eat meat, apart from anything they might kill on their occasional hunting trips.

Some keenly carnivorous monks found a way around this. They set their dogs on the pigs they were rearing for market and followed them in a mock chase through the monastery. Then they enjoyed the pork with a clear conscience.

If I can get as far as the chapel I can save my bacon.

TOURNAMENTS

When war was your business, tournaments provided a peacetime substitute. They developed out of a mounted free-for-all called a *mêlée*, a sort of fake battle designed to keep knights in training. There were few rules. Two lines of knights charged at each other with levelled lances, the object being to unhorse your opponent and capture him. Then he had to pay you a ransom, and his horse and harness (his most valuable possessions) were yours – or their equivalent in cash.

If you were a hard-up knight (and lots of younger sons were), tournaments were a good way of getting funds. Some knights became professional players, touring the tournament scene at home and abroad. The 12th-century English baron, William Marshal, fought in 500 bouts and was never beaten. He and a comrade (business partner?) took 203 knights in one season and employed two clerks to keep track of their winnings. William was well known as a reckless player. After one particularly hairy victory he was found with his head on a blacksmith's anvil, having his helmet battered off.

Tournaments were dangerous. People were often killed. At Nuys, near Cologne, in 1240, 60 knights and squires were reported dead, 'the most part suffocated by the dust'.

The Church condemned tournaments as hardly less sinful than unjust wars. In 1130 Pope Innocent III forbade Christian burial to anyone killed in one. In time, rules were introduced to make them safer.

Three types of tournament were recognised:

- those fought with real weapons

- those using 'arms of courtesy' designed not to wound: swords with no point or cutting edge; light lances with splayed tips that did not pierce armour

- a compromise form, with real weapons, in which the fight could be stopped at any time.

SOULS IN PERIL

Robert Manning, a 13th-century monk, warned that tournaments gave knights an excuse for all seven of the deadly sins:

1 **Pride** in one's strength

2 **Envy** of others

3 **Wrath** in the combat itself

4 **Sloth** in placing pleasure before devotion to God

5 **Covetousness** of opponents' horses and equipment

6 **Gluttony** at the feast

7 **Lechery** afterwards.

Proud? Me?

THE JOUST: THE KNIGHT OF THE BLACK STAG COMES A CROPPER

Later tournaments featured the joust, in which two knights tried to unhorse each other with their lances. In the 15th century a long barrier or 'tilt' was put between them, to stop an unseated rider being trampled by his opponent's horse.

By this time tournaments were so well regulated they were becoming pure pageantry.

- Day 1: Judges and contestants rode into the town in procession, and the banners of the chief knights were hung from the windows of their lodgings.

- Day 2: Noble ladies formally inspected a display of the contestants' helms, supposedly so they could denounce any knight guilty of an unchivalrous act.

- Day 3: A *chevalier d'honneur* (knight of honour) was chosen. During the contest he would carry a handkerchief upon a lance, and any knight he touched with it would be spared further attack.

- Day 4: The tournament proper took place, followed by the prize-giving ceremony.

- Each day ended with feasting, music and dancing.

WET DAY IN THE CASTLE

When long nights or bad weather kept people indoors they turned to chess (brought to Spain by the Moors), tables (a form of backgammon) or dice games. At feasts and around the fire they listened to songs and stories provided by the castle's resident minstrels or by the ragbag of wandering players and acrobats that knocked on castle gates and always flocked to weddings and celebrations.

A GRAND OCCASION

When the son of King Edward I of England was knighted in 1306, payments were made to 175 minstrels, mostly from outside the court, including a female dancer with the catchy stage name 'Pearl in the Egg.'*

> We do children's parties too.

It's possible that she was blind, and that her name means 'Pearl in the Eye', a rather poetic term for a cataract.

Perhaps the most extraordinary way of keeping visitors amused on a wet day was thought up by the fabulously rich 15th-century duke of Burgundy, Philip the Good. He had a gallery of 'surprises' installed at his favourite summer retreat, the Castle of Hesdin in Artois.

Ingenious hidden machinery made part of the floor collapse suddenly and drop unsuspecting visitors into a vat of feathers. When they touched a piece of furniture or went to look in a mirror they were squirted with water or got soot or flour dumped over them.

More sudden squirts of water shot up through the floor, which was especially entertaining when they went up ladies' skirts. We are not told whether the guests laughed as much as the duke.

Is this another of his jokes, or have I just had an accident?

CHAPTER EIGHT

CASTLES OF THE EAST

he castle idea – a secure residence strongly defended – is found worldwide, from pagan Latvian forts to the stockades of the first European settlers in America. In India its theory dates from at least the 4th century BC, when a statesman called Kautilya wrote the first of the many Indian treatises on military strategy. An Indian castle usually formed the highest point of a much bigger, walled, fortress-like area containing many buildings, and this in turn was often within a lower, walled township housing soldiers and craftsmen.

INDIAN CASTLES

Indian military treatises list 6 types of castle:

- the fortress surrounded by water

- the hill or mountain fortress

- the desert fortress

- the tree fortress, surrounded by forest

- the earth fortress, of which there are three types:

  - with earthen walls

  - with earth or stone walls half as wide as they are high

  - protected by fens or quicksands

- the fortress with men (a city fortress with a large garrison).

This meant that the castle was protected by several rings of walls. To enter the castle, an enemy had to negotiate zigzag routes and break through several gates. By tradition, a castle entry point should have seven protective gates. The great Rajput castle of Chittorgarh has seven gates at its main, western entrance, four at its eastern entrance, and one to the north.

Indian castle builders used all the defensive strategies known in the West – moats, strong gatehouses, curtain walls with flanking towers, battlements, machicolations – plus some of their own. Castle walls often seem much higher outside than within. This is because the lower parts of the outer wall only *look* man-made. A masonry facing has been put over the slope of solid rock on which the

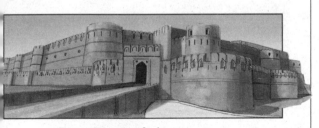

Red Fort of Agra, India

castle stands. This imitation walling could not be battered open or undermined.

On level ground, walls were sometimes protected by an Indian variation of the talus (see page 69). In place of a flat slope, it had a swelling profile like an upturned pudding basin (below). The 'hump' this produced meant that scaling ladders had to be based much further from the wall, and be much longer and lean more acutely, if they were to reach the top. This made ladders useless, as anything over 10 metres long would break under the weight of an assault party.

The impregnable entrance to
Kumbhalgarh

Moats, too, had an Indian flavour. Treatises recommended they should be planted with lotuses, lilies and creepers (good for entangling swimmers), and filled with specially bred crocodiles and poisonous snakes. Dry moats could be spiked with bamboo shoots cut at a sharp angle

Indian writers stress that fortifications must intimidate the enemy, by producing an overwhelming sense of wealth and power. Yet they should also impress by their beauty and grace. The gates should be elegantly ornamented, embossed with the emblem of the ruler and adorned with sculptures of lions, tigers, elephants or mythological beasts. The sixth gate of Gwalior Castle in Madhya Pradesh had a life-sized statue of an elephant ridden by a drover set before it (now, alas, removed).

Armies in India rarely used battering rams. They preferred elephants. By thrusting with their foreheads and working with their tusks and forelegs, elephants could destroy not just gates but masonry and brick walls as well.

ELEPHANTS

All castle gates had to be high enough for an elephant with a howdah on its back to pass through easily.

For protection against elephant attack, the doors were studded with sharp spikes of iron or teak – sometimes all over, sometimes just at the level of the elephant's forehead. But even this didn't always help. An infuriated elephant, provoked to a frenzy by flying stones and arrows, and driven into the gate at high speed, would break it in spite of the spikes.

Elephants were often decisive in winning a castle. Mahmud Ghazni, a Turkic conqueror of the 11th century, crashed through the gates of the castle of Taq with a famous elephant charge. When the castellan saw the elephants trampling his men to death, he surrendered the castle.

A panicking elephant could tip the scales either way. King Jayapala, founder of the Hindushahi dynasty, also pitted himself against Mahmud. Jayapala was on the point of victory when the elephant carrying his son took flight, and this turned the tide of battle. Jayapala threw himself onto a funeral pyre to avoid disgrace.

UNSTOPPABLE FORCE

Just as in the West, castles sometimes fell through treachery.

While Muhammad of Ghur, another Turkic invader, was besieging the castle of Uch in the 12th century, he invited the raja's wife to become the chief wife of his harem. Though she graciously declined the offer in favour of her daughter, she nevertheless had her husband put to death and surrendered the castle to Muhammad.

A nobler tale of an alluring wife involves Chittorgarh, one of the most famous castles in Rajasthan, dating largely from the 13th century. Today its ruins sprawl over nearly 3 square kilometres of hilltop. Once it was a majestic fortress crowned with temples and palaces and approached by a sharply zigzag route, blocked at intervals by seven gates. The gates were protected by a brilliant system of cross-walls, which prevented an enemy from bypassing any of them by cutting across.

THE TRAGIC SIEGE OF CHITTORGARH

In 1303 Ala-ud-din, Sultan of Delhi, led a conquering army into Rajasthan and set siege to Chittorgarh. Legend has it that his real motive was to gain the wife of its ruler, Prince Rattan Singh. She was said to be the most beautiful woman in the world. Her name was Padmini.

When the siege appeared to have reached a stalemate, Ala-ud-din tried a trick. He offered to withdraw his forces if he could be allowed a glimpse of the beautiful Padmini. This was unthinkable: no Rajput woman, let alone a princess, would ever show her face to a strange man.

However, the Rajputs were so exhausted they agreed to a compromise: Ala-ud-din could look at Padmini's reflection in a mirror. The princess stood with her back to him and looked into it. The Sultan was immediately smitten with burning love. When Rattan Singh escorted him courteously to the gate,

Ala-ud-din ordered his soldiers to seize him and drag him outside.

With the prince now his hostage, Ala-ud-din demanded his wife in exchange. The Rajputs thought up a scheme to outwit him. Padmini agreed to be his wife if she was allowed all the honour due to her rank. She demanded a procession of 700 covered palanquins for her ladies and maidservants. But, instead of a woman, each palanquin held an armed soldier and weapons for the six men who carried it. Do the arithmetic: that's 700 warriors plus 4,200 armed 'porters'. They freed the prince and his wife and fought their way back to the castle.

Ala-ud-din was furious and resumed the siege. The Rajputs had lost so many men in the rescue that it was clear that the castle was doomed. The women, led by Padmini, performed the rite of *jauhar* – self-burning. A pyre was lit in an underground chamber of the castle and the door was closed on them. Then the men galloped out of the gates to die in a last fight, or *saka*, from which none was allowed to return alive.

Death Before Dishonour

Before taking part in a saka, a Rajput washed and put on saffron robes (the colour sacred to Hinduism) and covered his head with a special turban, called a *mor*, studded with gems. He wore this turban only twice in his life: at his wedding, and in the saka. It symbolised both betrothal and the unity of warriors going to their death.

JAPANESE CASTLES

The earliest Japanese castles were simple hill-top defences of wattle and daub (woven sticks and mud plaster) that relied more on the natural defences of their site than on anything man-made. During the 13th and 14th centuries, when there was constant conflict between rival noble families, with bands of samurai (members of an aristocratic warrior class) at their command, bigger, stronger fortresses were built, housing large numbers of men and providing a residence for their *daimyo* or overlord.

These castles were made up of several wooden buildings within a defensive wall, which was also made of wood. Craftsmen and traders lived in a town outside the gates. Unlike their Western counterparts, the towns had no protective walls. Japan kept itself so isolated that its people had no fear of foreign enemies, and local foes would only aim for the castle. They spared the town for their own use later.

Himeji castle

Firearms appeared in Japan in 1543 and had an immediate effect on castle design. Azuki Castle, built in 1570, was given an immense stone base to withstand musket fire. It was also the first castle to have the tall, many-gabled central keep, called a *tenshu*, which gives later Japanese castles their characteristic outline. A tenshu was protected by a series of baileys, often one within another. The daimyo and his family lived in the tenshu, and his samurai in the baileys. The position of a samurai's living quarters was governed strictly by rank: the nearer to the tenshu, the greater the honour.

Above their stone bases, castle buildings continued to be made of wood. Apart from the risk of fire, wood was as practical as stone, as in Japan there was less need than in the West for castles to be cannon-proof. Heavy artillery was little used. Japan's foundries were more geared to casting temple bells, and importing foreign cannon was expensive. The preferred siege weapons were Chinese-style trebuchets and mangonels, which were aimed at people rather than buildings.

Japanese sieges were fought on completely different lines from those of the West. According to the samurai code, lurking in the safety of one's castle was shameful. A commander was supposed to lead his men out and fight the enemy in the open. By making a surprise sally he often gained the advantage.

Destroying the walls of a castle was not part of the besiegers' strategy. If they didn't succeed in open battle they cut off supply routes and waited for starvation to do the job. Sometimes this took so long that attackers built their own castles nearby.

In more settled times, from the 16th century onwards, a daimyo came to see his castle more as a means of impressing his rivals than of intimidating them. Buildings were given golden roof tiles and ornamented with sculptures of fish, cranes and tigers.

Fushimi castle was famous for its lavish decorations. Its tea-ceremony room was covered in gold leaf; it had a moon-viewing platform and elegant gardens.

It was dismantled after a bloody siege in 1600 and parts of it were used in later buildings. That's how the Yogen-in temple in Kyoto comes to have a bloodstained wooden *ceiling*: it used to be a floor at Fushimi.

Samurai battle armour

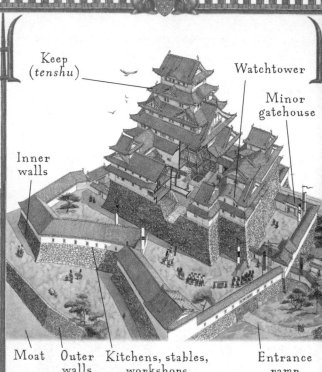

Keep
(*tenshu*)

Watchtower

Minor
gatehouse

Inner
walls

Moat

Outer
walls

Kitchens, stables,
workshops

Entrance
ramp

CASTLE OF THE WHITE HERON

The outstanding example of this type of very decorative castle is Himeji in Hyogo Prefecture. Begun in the 14th century, it is sometimes called 'White Heron Castle' because of its beautiful central tower which was finished in 1609. The white colour comes from the coating of plaster that was thought to protect buildings from fire. Fire was such a threat to these wooden buildings that anyone suspected of arson was burned alive. Himeji has never seen any fighting and is the best-preserved castle in Japan.

Attacking a castle by sea

🌀 KIKU'S WELL

Himeji castle has a famous well haunted by a beautiful servant girl called Okiku. Her master, the samurai Tesan Aoyama, tried to seduce her but she refused to have anything to do with him.

He tricked her into believing she had lost one of a set of ten precious plates. When she came to him to confess her carelessness he accused her of stealing the dish – an offence punishable by death – but offered to spare her if she became his mistress. When she still refused, the enraged samurai had her thrown to her death in the well.

Now her voice can be heard from the well, always counting from one to nine as she desperately checks the number of plates, followed by a terrible shriek as she realises the tenth is not there!

CHAPTER NINE

THE DECLINE OF THE CASTLE

In later medieval times the 'castle mentality' – the need to feel able to fight your own battles on your own doorstep – began to fade. Wars, which now involved hiring lots of professional soldiers, were becoming something that only kings could afford, and conflicts tended to be settled on the battlefield rather than by sieges.

The increasing use of gunpowder played a part in this. Relying on castle walls was no longer a safe strategy when cannon were firing at them.

FIREARMS

Gunpowder, an Eastern invention, seems to have reached the West in the 13th century. Edward I of England was using it at Stirling in Scotland in 1304, and Edward III had a number of 'gonnes' at the siege of Berwick Castle on the Scottish Borders in 1333.

Cannon were tricky things to be near in their early days. James II of Scotland went out with a bang at Roxburgh in 1460 when a bombard (a large front-loading cannon) exploded next to him. James II's collection of guns included the huge bombard known as Mons Meg, which was made in 1449 and is now preserved at Edinburgh Castle.

All this meant the gradual sidelining of castles as a means of defence, though this happened at different rates in various parts of Europe.

When new castles were built, their convenience was often considered as carefully as, or more carefully than, their defence. But if they couldn't be defended, were they really castles?

Fourteenth-century Bodiam Castle in Sussex, England, is a good example of a 'doubtful' castle. It has the right ingredients: gatehouse, battlements, portcullises and drawbridge. It stands in the middle of an impressive moat. But the site is on a gentle slope, so the moat could easily be drained by breaking its retaining bank. A stroll round shows up more weak spots. Two of its outside walls have large windows, and the walls themselves are only a few feet (a couple of metres) thick. There is an impressive gatehouse at the front but the postern gate at the rear has hardly any protection.

So why build a castle at all? Wouldn't it have been pleasanter to live in a large house or a modest palace? It seems that a castle was the 14th-century status symbol. It was what great lords had always built, and if you were only recently great you wanted one of your own.

Sir Edward Dallingridge, Bodiam's builder, was an upwardly mobile knight. His family had improved on humble origins by some good marriages. Edward was the first member to be knighted. He made a fortune as a mercenary, rampaging through France during what is now called the Hundred Years' War, looting villages and holding people to ransom (he sold their armour for £400 a suit.) He came back with enough plunder to build himself something impressive and married an heiress whose property included the manor of Bodiam.

Sir Edward received a 'licence to crenellate' (royal permission to put up a building with battlements) from Richard II in 1385, on the grounds that a castle at Bodiam would be 'in the defence of the country against our enemies' (the French). This is rather fishy, as Bodiam is some way from the sea and not in a good defensive position: it's overlooked by higher ground, being halfway down a hill. Perhaps its defensive potential was exaggerated by the crafty knight.

It seems that the real aim of Sir Edward's castle was to impress. It told the world that the family inside expected obedience and respect.

Bodiam was certainly a home to be proud of. As well as the usual great hall and a built-in kitchen, pantry and buttery, there was a suite of private rooms on the ground floor for Sir Edward and his family and guest chambers in the four towers, each with window seats and an en-suite toilet.

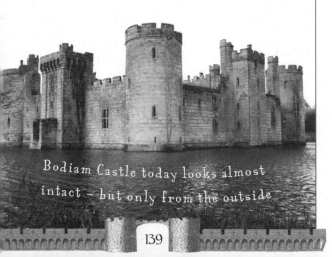

Bodiam Castle today looks almost intact – but only from the outside

By the 17th century, cannon were powerful enough to smash their way through castle walls, and sieges went out of fashion. The last truly 'medieval' siege in Britain was at Raglan Castle in Wales in 1646, during the Civil War.

The castle belonged to the marquis of Worcester. His ancestors had spent 200 years improving it and it was now one of the finest in Britain. The marquis was living there quietly in retirement after a long career serving the Crown. When the war came he was a staunch Royalist, supplying the king with funds, though at nearly 60 he felt too old for battle. However, battle came to him. When almost all the Royalist strongholds had fallen, the marquis found 1,500 Roundhead troops outside his walls with a demand for surrender.

His reply was courteous:

'We will, to the last man, sell our lives as dear as we can, and this not out of obstinacy or any ill affection, but merely to preserve that honour that I desire should attend me with death.'

The siege lasted over two months. The Roundheads pounded Raglan with up to 60 cannon shots a day, but their culverins (cannon firing weights of up to 20 lb / 9 kg) could topple the battlements but not the castle walls. Seven weeks into the siege, a force of 2,000 extra Roundheads arrived, and still the marquis went on defending a peaceable Englishman's right to live in his home unmolested. The end came when he was faced with a truly terrible enemy: Roaring Meg!

Roundhead artillery

Roaring Meg

Meg was the most frightening weapon imaginable in the 17th century. She was a big, squat mortar designed to lob missiles over walls rather than at them. She delivered 200 lb (90 kg) grenades packed with gunpowder. When they exploded, shrapnel flew in all directions, killing or maiming large numbers of people.

Roaring Meg is now on display at Goodrich Castle in Herefordshire. (She was originally made for the siege of Goodrich, which ended just 3 weeks before that of Raglan.)

The old marquis did not put Meg to the test. He wasn't prepared to shed the lives of his family and all around him in an inevitable defeat. The Roundhead commander promised him safe-conduct, and he surrendered on 19 August 1646. Parliament put him in the Tower and he died the same year.

The Raglan siege was the last gasp of the military castle. After this, if there was any chance that a castle could be put to unwelcome military use it was 'slighted', which meant that its walls were broken through and the roof stripped off to let the wind and rain finish the job.

Few castles were utterly destroyed. Their walls were so strong, they cost more to demolish than their stone was worth. They fell into ruin and, as time passed and they gently crumbled into the landscape, people began to regard them in a new light. They were relics of 'olden times', mysterious and romantic...

ROMANTIC RUINS

The 18th century invented the term 'picturesque' to describe the sort of scene where a glimpse of ruins gives the finishing touch.

If you had the land and money, you could create a picturesque landscape in your own grounds. To complete it, the logical thing was to build yourself a new ruin – and people did.

And while you're spending money on a ruin, why not make it useful? This sensible idea led to some very nonsensical buildings. The romantic fragment of a medieval chamber proved on a closer look to be the false front of a cattleshed; the mouldering castle tower and the labourer's cottage apparently built from its stones were both put up yesterday.

DECISIONS, DECISIONS

A hot topic for discussion in the 18th century was what type of ruin you should build. Many favoured Greek ruins as being the most beautiful. Others strongly objected to them in an English landscape because the Greeks never built here.

Ruins also had to inspire the right sort of thoughts. As one writer put it: 'Grecian ruins suggest the triumph of barbarity over taste; a gloomy and discouraging thought,' while 'Gothic [medieval] ruins exhibit the triumph of time over strength, a melancholy but not displeasing thought.'

So castle ruins won the day!

A Gothic cowshed

LUSCOMBE CASTLE OR SHAM?

THE COUNTRY—HOUSE CASTLE

Gracious living in a castle was an attractive idea to lots of people, provided they could be comfortable. The castle's romantic associations – noble names, chivalry, armour and tournaments – appealed to people who would have liked to have that sort of thing in the family. They got their architect to run them up a modest castle with French windows, conservatory and direct access to the garden. Prettily battlemented Luscombe Castle in Devon (opposite), built in 1799, is a good example.

To some, this seemed rather like cheating. 'The castle style requires massive walls, with very small windows,' pontificated landscape designer Humphry Repton; 'Its correct imitation must produce the effect of a prison.' By which he meant that making a house look like a castle was like trying to square the circle; it just wouldn't do.

Nevertheless, clients were prepared to give it a go. Penrhyn Castle in Gwynedd, North Wales, was built in the 1820s in the Norman style for the Pennant family, who had made their fortune from Jamaican sugar and Welsh slate quarries.

Penrhyn is medieval through and through, with Norman windows and two keeps, all rather sombre and forbidding. Prince Hermann von Pückler-Muskau, a much-travelled German nobleman, visited it in 1828. He noted that every entrance had 'a fortress-like gate with a portcullis that frowns on the intruder' and that the dining hall was copied from the keep at Rochester (of 1130!).

'What could then be accomplished only by a mighty monarch is now executed by a simple country gentleman whose father very likely sold cheeses. So times do change,' he mused.

King George IV, well known for his building appetite, caught the enthusiasm for old castles. In the 1820s he decided to give Windsor Castle a make-over on a grand scale. He and his architect Jeffry Wyatville turned the lopsided jumble of centuries into the perfect 'medieval' castle. George persuaded Parliament to vote him £300,000 to pay for the work.

Nothing too flashy, mind. I'm a man of simple tastes.

⊞INDSOR

Windsor castle, the British Queen's official residence, is the largest inhabited castle in the world. It was begun by William the Conqueror and most English monarchs had a go at extending it. In the Civil War it fell to the Roundheads and served as a military headquarters, which did it no good. A proposal to demolish it was defeated in Parliament by only one vote.

Charles II gave it new apartments and a grand avenue of elm trees (now chestnuts), but it then fell slowly into disrepair and by the 18th century it was barely habitable.

In 1811 King George III became mentally unbalanced and had to be kept in the castle for his own safety. During the last nine years of his life he seldom left his apartments there.

Wyatville made Windsor Castle symmetrical and majestic. He raised its curtain towers to a uniform height and put Gothic façades and battlements on the more recent bits. He added height to the great Round Tower with a false upper storey, making a dramatic silhouette visible for miles.

No detail that would help a picturesque effect was overlooked. He left holes in the masonry for jackdaws and starlings to nest in, 'a very tasteful provision by which the castle has been made to retain its ancient effect'.

In France a similar movement to restore medieval buildings was spearheaded by scholarly architect Eugène Viollet-le-Duc. He didn't believe in just putting them back the way they were, but in supplying the parts their medieval builders had probably planned to build but hadn't got round to. As a result his work is almost too complete. His magnificent restoration of Pierrefonds Castle in the département of Oise is chilling in its stony perfection – no holes left for the jackdaws.

LUDWIG II DIDN'T LIKE TO DO THINGS BY HALVES

Castle lovers must be grateful to Viollet-le-Duc for one thing. It was through seeing his work at Pierrefonds in 1861 that King Ludwig II of Bavaria was bitten by the castle-building bug. He got the frenzy very badly, to the despair of his ministers and the ruin of his finances, but among his crazy creations is the magical Neuschwanstein (left), rising like a dream castle from a breathtaking mountaintop site in the Bavarian Alps. Its fairytale turrets are better known than any other castle skyline, being the inspiration for all the castles of Disneyland.

In America there are no hang-ups about a castle having to look medieval. It's the attitude that counts. Hearst Castle in California is the dream-creation of newspaper baron William Randolph Hearst, built on a 40,000-acre (16,000-hectare) ranch left him by his father.

It was an idea that grew and grew (it started as a bungalow), inspired by the castles of Europe and aiming to rival them. Work began in 1919 but Hearst constantly changed his mind, tearing down buildings whenever an idea seized him. The castle was still unfinished when he died in 1951.

Its façade is modelled on a 16th-century Spanish cathedral, with interiors filled with art, antiques and entire rooms brought over from the great houses of Europe. Part of a real Roman temple graces an outdoor pool. There was a movie theatre lined with rare books, an airfield, and the world's largest private zoo.

The castle is now a historical monument open to the public, so it can't challenge Windsor Castle's claim to be the largest *inhabited* castle in the world. In Hearst's day, maybe it could.

CHAPTER TEN

CASTLES OF THE IMAGINATION

'Castles in the air' is the name we give to projects that have no firm foundations in reality. That exactly describes the host of imaginary castles that poets and novelists have given us – the fantastic, the festive, the sinister (lot of those).

Fairytales have a good range of castles, from Sleeping Beauty's, entangled in briers, to Bluebeard's where it doesn't do to take too close a look. As to the Ogre's castle that Jack found at the top of the beanstalk – what could be more of a castle in the air than that?

ᛏO BOLDLY GO...

For a truly blood-bloodcurdling fairytale castle you can't beat the one that belonged to the mysterious Mr Fox, which had this ominous motto over its door:

BE BOLD, BE BOLD,
BUT NOT TOO BOLD,
LEST THY HEART'S BLOOD
TURN TO COLD

No idle warning! The heroine had a severed finger thrown down the neck of her bodice.*

* *It wasn't* her *finger, and all was well in the end.*

At least Mr Fox's castle was up front about itself. Top prize in the 'most deceptive castle' category must go to Macbeth's castle in Shakespeare's play – site of one of literature's nastiest murders. Victims-to-be, King Duncan and his companion Banquo, are smitten by its charm.

Duncan: This castle hath a pleasant seat; the air
  Nimbly and sweetly recommends itself
  Unto our gentle senses.

Banquo agrees: 'Heaven's breath smells wooingly here,' and goes on enthusiastically for several more lines.

Both are happy to spend the night there – but we know better![1]

1. In the play (but not in real life), Macbeth murders Duncan while he sleeps, and later hires thugs to kill Banquo and his son – but the son escapes and eventually becomes the ancestor of King James I.

Some airy castles have very familiar names, but there's surprisingly little evidence of what they looked like. Camelot, for instance, was first mentioned as King Arthur's castle by the 12th-century French poet Chrétien de Troyes, but he has nothing to say of it except that it was 'molt riche' (very magnificent).

Later French versions of the Arthurian legends say only that Camelot stood on a river and was surrounded by woods and hills. Even Sir Thomas Malory, who wove together lots of Arthurian sources in his *Morte d'Arthur*, gives no description of it as a place (apart from thinking it was at Winchester), though he has lots to tell of its adventures. The castle itself has to be found in our imaginations.

If we need any help, the job has been done for us by the 1967 film *Camelot*, with Richard Harris and Vanessa Redgrave, based on an earlier musical. The film used the late 15th-century Spanish castle of Coca near Segovia as a setting – a magnificent building, though rather Moorish-looking for the residence of a legendary British king.

Malory has more to say of the Castle of the Holy Grail, which housed the sacred chalice that only the purest and noblest knight could look upon. He calls the castle Corbin or Corbenic. It belonged to the mysterious 'maimed king' whose wound could not be healed. According to Sir Lancelot, its tower was the fairest he had ever seen. Its gate, which stood open, was guarded by two lions and a dwarf.

The goings-on there were wondrous. Sir Lancelot freed a lady from a curse that had imprisoned her in the tower for many years in boiling water. Sir Bors, who spent the night there, called it the Castle Adventurous – an understatement on his part, after sleeping, or trying to sleep, in a room where an invisible hand wounded him with a flaming spear, arrows were mysteriously rained on him and he had to fight a lion and behead it.

The Round Table

According to castle etiquette, diners at long tables were seated in order of importance. It's said that Arthur's followers came to blows one Yuletide over their placing. The problem was solved by making a round table at which everyone could feel equal.

In later versions of the Arthurian legends, the Round Table came to symbolise the ideal of knightly chivalry.

There is an actual round table – or at least its top – hanging on a wall in Winchester Castle. It is 5.5 metres across and weighs a tonne and a quarter; at least twelve oak trees were used to make it. It was probably made for one of the round-table tournaments, popular in the Middle Ages, that imitated the glories of Camelot. Dendrochronology dates it to the 13th century – much too late for Arthur's use – and it was repainted in the time of Henry VIII.

Shakespeare again: spooky and tragic, the castle of Elsinore. Modern productions of *Hamlet* often use a minimalist set of movable ramps and screens, but anyone lucky enough to have seen the 1948 film that Lawrence Olivier made and starred in knows exactly what its haunted, mist-wreathed battlements and guilt-ridden interiors are like. (Christopher Lee, who went on to become a celebrated horror-film actor, has an uncredited role as a spear carrier in the film.)

Another famous castle that owes more to our imaginings than to description is John Bunyan's Doubting Castle in *The Pilgrim's Progress* (1678).

Christian and his companion Hopeful leave the rough and difficult path leading to the Celestial City in favour of a short-cut through By-Path-Meadow. Narrowly escaping a deep pit that has just swallowed up a man called Vain-Confidence, they get lost in the dark and decide to sleep till morning, not knowing that they are in the fields of the grim and surly Giant Despair.

The giant imprisons them in his fortress, Doubting Castle, in 'a very dark Dungeon, nasty and stinking to the spirits of these two men. Here they lay, from Wednesday morning till Saturday night, without one bit of bread, or drop to drink, or any light.'

There is a strong flavour of the tougher kind of fairytale in the way Bunyan tells the story. The giant is an evil bully and his wife, Diffidence (meaning 'lack of Christian faith'), is even worse. The giant is browbeaten by his wife and has to ask her three times on three successive nights how he ought to treat the prisoners.

On the first night she tells him to beat them with a crab-tree cudgel.

On the second night she tells him to drive them to suicide. Hopeful manages to dissuade Christian from this.

On the third night she tells him to take them into the castle yard and show them the bones and skulls of the victims he has killed.

The couple's conversations take place in bed at night. One imagines them in their nightcaps, mumbling at each other because their false teeth are out (though they wouldn't have had false teeth in the 17th century, would they?).

Giant Despair
by Frederick Barnard, from an 1894 edition of *The Pilgrim's Progress*

The 18th-century taste for crumbling ruins produced the horror castle novel, with ghostly monks and family curses. Horace Walpole set the ball rolling with his *Castle of Otranto*. Anne Radcliffe's 1794 *Mysteries of Udolpho* was the peak of the craze. It sent young ladies swooning all the way to the circulating library.

Castle spine-chillers were sent up mercilessly by Jane Austen in *Northanger Abbey*. Its 18-year-old heroine, Catherine, reads almost nothing else.

'My dearest Catherine [a friend asks], have you got on with *Udolpho*?'

'I have been reading it ever since I woke and am got to the black veil.'

'Oh! I would not tell you what is behind the black veil for the world! Are you not wild to know?'

'Do not tell me. I know it must be a skeleton; I am sure it is Laurentina's skeleton. Oh! I am delighted with the book!'

Naturally, when Catherine's invited to stay in a house that's part-medieval, she assumes that her host has murdered his wife, or, even more likely, is keeping her locked up in the Gothic wing. When the very dull truth gets out, poor Catherine is overcome with embarrassment.

Horror castles were revived with a vengeance in Bram Stoker's 1897 novel *Dracula*, the first and best of all vampire stories. Dracula's castle in the Transylvanian mountains has all the trappings: 'frowning walls,' 'dark window openings', 'rattling chains', 'the clanking of massive bolts' – plus rather more blood than its predecessors.

Bram Stoker never went to Transylvania (part of Romania) and didn't have a real castle in mind, but he seems to have based the character of Count Dracula on an outstandingly cruel 15th-century Romanian prince, Vlad III of Wallachia, known as Vlad Dracula,[1] and sometimes as Vlad the Impaler. (The latter nickname came from his habit of spitting his enemies on stakes.) He was a capable ruler despite his faults, and is remembered in Romania as a national hero for driving out the invading Ottoman Turks.

1. Dracula *means 'Son of the Dragon'; his father was a knight of the Order of the Dragon. But it also means 'Son of the Devil'.*

DRACULA'S CASTLE

DRACULA'S REAL HOME?

Bran Castle in Romania is associated with Vlad Dracula (he's known to have stayed there), and this has encouraged the Romanian tourist industry to promote it as 'Dracula's Castle'. It certainly looks the part, rising from a forested crag overlooking a mountain pass.

Bran dates from the 14th century, though much altered and restored. It became a royal residence in the 20th century, was seized by the Communists and later restored to its owners, who have made it a museum dedicated to local history and to the memory of Queen Marie of Romania (1875–1938), who lived there – no mention of vampires!

Bran Castle

The fictional castle to out-castle all others must surely be Mervyn Peake's Gormenghast, which first astounded readers in 1946. Three volumes (more were planned) tell of the struggles of its 77th earl, young Titus Groan, to escape the asphyxiating rituals of his ancestral home.

Gormenghast Castle is so vast, its inhabitants cannot grasp its extent. It's mostly ruinous: its dank corridors and decaying halls are moss-encrusted, ivy-choked, hung with 'swathes of cobwebs like fly-filled hammocks'. No wonder the people who live in it are stranger than their names: Prunesquallor, Swelter or Flannelcat. But this is no joke castle. It breeds insane ambition, murder and revenge. Great stuff, if rather wordy. Addicts love it.

It's a relief after this to come to today's most popular imaginary castle, the resplendent Hogwarts, an ancient lordly residence adapted at some time past (we're not told when) to accommodate Britain's premier school of wizardry.

The film versions of the castle's halls, courts and stairways are too familiar to need describing. Several places were stitched together to create them, including:

- Gloucester cathedral cloisters (the school's corridors, and also the setting for the talking pictures in *The Philosopher's Stone*[1] and the overflowing bathrooms in *The Chamber of Secrets*)

- Durham cathedral (for one of the classrooms)

- Lacock Abbey in Wiltshire (interior scenes)

- The Great Hall of Christ Church, Oxford (the dining hall)

- Duke Humphrey's Library (part of the Bodleian Library), Oxford (for library scenes)

- Divinity Schools, Oxford (the sanatorium)

- The grounds at Hogwarts are largely those of Alnwick Castle in Northumberland.

1. Sorcerer's Stone *in the USA and India.*

Rochester castle,
Kent, England

EXPLORING OUR CASTLE HERITAGE

CHAPTER ELEVEN

NEW USES FOR OLD CASTLES

he best days of the castle may be over, but don't write them off as just a lot of fossilised tourist attractions. They still have their uses.

Where's their TV aerial?

171

DEFENDING THE REALM

When Britain faced the threat of a German invasion in World War II, it needed defence points on the south coast. There was a castle to hand, at just the spot where invasion has always been most likely – at Pevensey, where William the Conqueror had landed.

The remains of Pevensey Castle's massive walls now came into their own, refortified as an observation and command post.

Its towers were fitted up to provide sleeping quarters; machine-gun emplacements were built in the keep and along the walls; the south-west entrance was closed with a blockhouse for anti-tank weapons and an entirely new tower was added to the eastern wall.

This wasn't just a half-baked, 'Dad's Army' idea – postwar evidence showed that this was exactly the route the Germans had planned for their march on London.

So This is Colditz!

Colditz Castle, a grim stronghold atop a hill in Saxony, Germany, has been put to many uses:

- Begun in 1158 by Frederick Barbarossa, it served as the watchtower of the German emperors.

- In the 15th century it became the royal residence of the Electors of Saxony.

- In 1803 it was turned into a workhouse.

- From 1829 to 1924 it was a mental hospital for the 'incurably insane'.

- In 1933 the Nazis turned it into a political prison for Communists, Jews and other people they considered 'undesirable'.

- In World War II it was the notorious prisoner-of-war camp for Allied officers who were repeat escapers from less secure places.

- In 1945 the Russians imprisoned non-Communists there. Later it became an old people's home.

- Empty and in disrepair since 1996, it has recently been transformed into an escape museum, youth hostel and holiday centre.

FANCY HONEYMOONING IN A PRISON?

Oxford Castle, dating back to a motte and bailey job of 1081, had been used as a prison since the 13th century and officially became HM Prison Oxford in 1888.

More recently it has been a popular film set, featuring in *The Italian Job* and *A Fish Called Wanda*, and in the TV series *Inspector Morse*, *Bad Girls* and *The Bill*.

Closed in 1996, the prison has now been revamped as a heritage complex, with performance venues, open courtyards for markets, and guided tours of the buildings.

The prison block is now a hotel, the Malmaison Oxford, describing itself as a 'stunning boutique hotel' with guest rooms in the converted cells. The 'Love Suite Love' package offers champagne on ice, aromatic oils and candlelight. Things have certainly changed since Matilda was lowered over the walls in her white nightie (see pages 92–93)!

Oxford is the first UK prison to be turned into a hotel. An idea that's likely to catch on?

SPOOKY CASTLES

Let's not forget the ghosts. They're regular users of old castles and no castle book is complete without some. Here are five memorable ones:

1 Glamis Castle in Scotland is haunted by the sounds of a furious row which the first Lord of Glamis had with the devil. He was a gambling man with a quick temper, and having no-one to play cards with one night he said he'd sooner play with the devil than no-one. The devil turned up; the Lord kept losing to him and ranted and raved so loudly that a servant knocked to see if all was well. While the Lord went to the door the devil disappeared, taking, it is said, the Lord's soul with him.

2 Dragsholm Castle in Denmark has the ghost of James, Earl of Bothwell, third husband of Mary Queen of Scots. When Scotland got too hot for him after the murder of Mary's second husband, Darnley, he went to Scandinavia. The King of Denmark clapped him in prison at Dragsholm on

I didnae do it!
It wisnae me!

suspicion of the murder. The pillar he was chained to is still there, and around it in the floor is a circular groove he is said to have worn with his feet during the last ten years of his life which he spent in the prison.

3 Malahide, the oldest inhabited castle in Ireland, boasts five ghosts. The pick of the bunch are:

• 15th-century Sir Walter Hussey, who wanders about groaning and pointing to a spear-wound that killed him in battle (on his wedding day!) His bride then married a rival and he can't get over it.

• Miles Corbett, who held the castle in Cromwellian times. He signed Charles I's death warrant and was hanged, drawn and quartered for it later. His ghost roams Malahide as a figure in armour that falls into four pieces before your eyes.

4 **The Tower of London** is packed with ghosts with famous names, too many to mention. One not so famous appeared to a sentry on guard outside the Jewel House in 1816. He saw a ghostly bear advancing on him. It literally frightened him to death, for he reportedly died a few days later.

5 Ghosts, of course, can't be trusted to appear. They're only as reliable as the people who see them. An old man interviewed by antiquarian H. Jenner in 1867 reported seeing the ghosts of King Arthur's soldiers drilling at **Castle-an-Dinas** in Cornwall. He particularly remembered 'the glancing of the moonbeams on their muskets'! (Think about it.)

☖OURISM

Today's biggest users of castles are the tourists, so the last word should go to them. A Dutch website has done a customer survey and rated the top ten European castles according to the level of visitor satisfaction. Here's the list:

1 All-out winner: France's **Carcassonne**, a complete 12th-century city-fortress (restored by Viollet-le-Duc in the 19th century)

2 **Krak des Chevaliers** in Syria (Crusader-built, so it counts as European)

3 **The Tower of London**

4 Poland's **Malbork**, stunning 13th-century fortress of the Teutonic Knights, claiming to be the biggest brick-built castle in the world

5 Switzerland's **Château de Chillon**, a romantic 12th-century castle on Lake Geneva, subject of a famous poem by Byron

6 **Castel del Monte**, Emperor Frederick II's 13th-century castle-cum-hunting-lodge in Apulia, southern Italy

7 **Dover Castle**, England

Harlech

8 **Harlech Castle**, Wales

9 Wales again, scoring with **Caernarfon Castle**

10 **Château Gaillard**, Normandy (which might have scored higher if it weren't such a ruin).

Castle buffs will spot at once that something's missing from this list. Where's Germany's hugely popular Neuschwanstein, the perfect fairytale castle? The compilers wouldn't allow it because it isn't a proper medieval castle. You can see their point: it was only begun in the 1860s. If it had been in the running it would probably have made first place.

Glossary

armoury A place where armour and weapons are kept.

bailey The outer enclosure of a castle; later, any enclosure within a castle's series of walls.

barracks Lodgings for soldiers.

bastion A heavily defended tower or fortification.

belfry A mobile wooden tower used to get troops to the top of a wall.

Byzantines The Christian people of the eastern part of the old Roman empire, whose capital was Constantinople (formerly Byzantium, now Istanbul).

capon A castrated cock.

castellan The governor or constable of a castle.

cat Another name for a battering ram.

chapel A place for Christian worship, often part of a larger building such as a castle.

chivalry The behaviour expected of a knight: courage, fairness, good manners.

chronicler The writer of a chronicle – a description of historical events in the order in which they occurred.

circulating library A commercial library from which anyone could borrow books.

Civil War The conflict in England, from 1642 to 1651, between Royalists who supported the monarchy and Parliamentarians who wished Parliament to control government.

concentric castle A castle with two or more complete circuits of walls one within the other.

constable The commander of a castle.

countermine A tunnel dug from a castle by defenders in order to break into the attackers' mine.

crossbow A powerful bow with a mechanism for tightening and releasing the string.

Crusades A series of military expeditions, from the 11th to the 13th centuries, in which Christians from Europe tried to recapture the Biblical Holy Land from the Muslims.

dendrochronology The dating of wooden objects by examining the annual growth rings of their timber.

donjon The Old French word for the tower or main building of a castle (later called the **keep**).

drawbridge A hinged bridge that could be drawn up to prevent an enemy crossing the moat.

dubbing The ceremonial blow on the shoulder that signifies that the recipient is now a knight.

dysentery A bacterial infection of the intestines.

elevation of the Host The point during the celebration of Mass when the priest raises aloft the sacred wafer, representing the body of Christ.

eunuch A castrated man.

excommunicate To cut someone off from all communion with the Church.

feudal system A modern name for the system of government in medieval Europe in which the king gave land to lords (barons) and expected loyalty in return. The lords gave land to lesser lords, and so on.

flanking towers Towers projecting from a wall, allowing defenders to fire along the wall from arrow slits in the tower sides.

gambeson A padded tunic of thick cloth or leather, worn under armour.

garrison A body of soldiers stationed in a certain place in order to defend it.

gatehouse A fortified entrance to a castle.

Greek fire A highly explosive mixture used in the medieval equivalent of a grenade.

hauberk A sleeved tunic of chain mail or leather.

helm A helmet entirely enclosing the head, which often bore a decorative crest to identify the wearer.

Holy Land, The Another name for Palestine, an area of the Middle East that roughly corresponds to present-day Israel.

hostage A person who is held prisoner, either to force his or her friends to pay a ransom or as security for an agreement (if the agreement is broken, the hostage may be killed). The taking of hostages was considered a normal part of medieval warfare.

howdah A seat, often with a canopy over it, carried on the back of an elephant.

Hundred Years' War A long-running conflict, from 1337 to 1453, between France and England, over the English monarch's claim to the throne of France.

keep A word used from the 16th century to describe the **donjon** – the tower or main part of a castle.

lay people All those who are not in holy orders.

Lent The period between Ash Wednesday and Easter in which Christians forgo certain pleasures, such as eating meat, in memory of Christ's fasting in the wilderness.

machicolations Battlemented stone platforms built out from the upper part of a wall, with holes in the floor through which defenders could drop material on attackers immediately below.

Mamluks A warrior class in Muslim countries, originally consisting of ex-slaves converted to Islam.

mercenary A soldier who fights for pay, not out of loyalty to a lord or ruler.

mine A tunnel dug under a wall to weaken the foundations and bring it down.

missile Any kind of weapon that is thrown or fired from a bow or a gun.

moat A big ditch, usually water-filled.

Moors A Muslim people from North Africa who conquered Spain in the 8th century and ruled parts of it until the 15th century.

mortar A cannon with a short, wide barrel, that can be pivoted to fire at a high angle.

mullein A plant of the figwort family, the most common form having woolly leaves and tall stems of small yellow flowers.

Normans A people of Scandinavian origin who settled in northern France. They conquered England in 1066.

overlord A lord who has authority over lesser lords.

palanquin A chair with a canopy, carried by bearers.

pallet A thin straw mattress.

pilgrimage A journey to worship at a holy site.

pitch A tarry substance.

portcullis A heavy grating of metal or metal-clad wood that could be dropped down vertical grooves to block a gate.

postern A rear entrance to a castle or a walled town.

raja An Indian prince.

rampart A mound of earth forming a defensive barrier, usually with a wall on top.

ransom Money paid for the release of a prisoner.

relieving force An army sent to give help, such as by driving off the besiegers of a castle.

ricochet To hit glancingly and rebound.

Roundheads Supporters of the Parliamentarians in the English Civil War, so called because they wore their hair very short.

sarcocolla A resinous gum from Arabia and Persia.

Saxons A people of Germanic origin who settled in Britain from the 5th century onwards.

sheriff The monarch's representative in a shire (an administrative district).

shrapnel Fragments of metal from an exploded bomb or shell.

slighting The partial demolition of a castle, to prevent it being used for defence.

supply chain The arrangements made to get food and equipment to an army fighting away from its base.

talus An additional sloping front along the lower part of a wall.

tartar Salts of tartaric acid.

trencher A flat wooden plate or a slice of stale bread on which food was served.

truckle bed A low bed on wheels, which can be stored under a larger bed when it is not in use.

vassal A person holding land from a superior, in return for performing certain duties.

ward Another name for **bailey**.

workhouse A place where the poor were given food and shelter in return for doing manual work.

wormwood A plant of the *Artemisia* genus, with silvery-grey, very acrid-smelling leaves.

yeoman An attendant ranking between a squire and a page.

Timeline of castle history

9th–10th centuries Timber castles appear in north-western France.

Late 10th century Earliest known stone keeps appear in the Loire valley, France.

1051 First castles in England recorded.

1078 William the Conqueror begins building the White Tower, London, though timber castles remain the norm during the 11th century.

1095 Pope Urban II preaches the First Crusade.

1099 Crusaders capture Jerusalem.

12th century Increasing use of stone in castle building.

1110 Crusaders take over Krak des Chevaliers, Syria.

1142 Siege of Oxford; escape of Matilda. Hospitallers take over ownership of Krak des Chevaliers.

Later 12th century New forms of keep, circular or polygonal, are tried.

1147–1149 Second Crusade.

1158 Emperor Frederick Barbarossa builds Colditz Castle, Germany.

1165 Henry II of England builds Orford Castle with a polygonal keep.

1179–1214 English kings Henry II and John build Dover Castle, the first in Europe to have a double ring of defensive walls.

1189–1192 Third Crusade.

1190s Richard I of England adds a large additional bailey to the Tower of London.

1196–1198 Richard I builds Château Gaillard, France.

13th century Concentric walls take over from the keep

13th century Concentric walls take over from the keep as the castle's strongest line of defence. Firearms appear for the first time in the West. Chittorgarh, in India, dates largely from this century.

1202–1204 Fourth Crusade ends in the looting of Christian Constantinople.

1204 French king Philip Augustus captures Château Gaillard.

1215 Siege of Rochester Castle.

1238 Henry III extends the Tower of London's defensive walls northwards and eastwards, doubling the castle's area.

c.1240 Louis IX of France extends the fortifications of Carcassonne.

1271 Muslims capture Krak des Chevaliers.

1275–1281 Edward I of England, one of the foremost castle-builders of his time, expands the Tower of London into a concentric fortress with a triple gatehouse defence.

1283 Edward I begins a big castle-building programme in Wales with Conwy, Harlech and Caernarfon.

1291 Destruction of the port of Acre marks the end of Crusader kingdoms in the Holy Land.

14th century Castle design reaches its fullest development in northern Europe.

1337 Outbreak of the Hundred Years' War between France and England.

1346 Himeji Castle, Japan, built.

1385 Bodiam Castle built.

15th century Castles figure less in military strategy as conflicts tend to be settled on the battlefield rather than by sieges.

1486 Man Mandir palace, Gwalior, begun in India.
(Gwalior had been fortified since AD 773.)

16th century Increasingly, lords prefer to build
themselves comfortable houses rather than castles.

1600 Siege of Fushimi Castle, Japan.

1608 Himeji Castle, Japan, rebuilt.

1642 Outbreak of Civil War gives English castles a
new lease of life.

1646 Siege of Raglan Castle.

1649 English Parliament orders the demolition of
castles. When this proves too expensive, their
'slighting' (partial demolition) is ordered.

18th century Castle ruins are considered 'picturesque'.
Medieval or 'Gothic' architectural styles are revived.

1799 Luscombe Castle built (a house in disguise).

1820–1830 King George IV restores Windsor Castle.

1820–1845 Penrhyn Castle built in Norman style.

1861 Viollet-le-Duc starts restoring Pierrefonds Castle.

1869 King Ludwig II of Bavaria begins
Neuschwanstein.

1919–1947 William Randolph Hearst creates and
recreates Hearst Castle, California.

2006 Oxford Castle, formerly a prison, becomes a
luxury hotel and visitor attraction.

2007 Colditz Castle becomes a youth hostel and escape
museum.

Index

Very Peculiar Histories™

The Blitz
David Arscott
ISBN: 978-1-907184-18-5

London
Jim Pipe
ISBN: 978-1-907184-26-0

Brighton
David Arscott
ISBN: 978-1-906714-89-5

Rations
David Arscott
ISBN: 978-1-907184-25-3

Castles
Jacqueline Morley
ISBN: 978-1-907184-48-2

Scotland
Fiona Macdonald

Vol. 1: From ancient times
to Robert the Bruce
ISBN: 978-1-906370-91-6

Christmas
Fiona Macdonald
ISBN: 978-1-907184-50-5

Vol. 2: From the Stewarts
to modern Scotland
ISBN: 978-1-906714-79-6

Great Britons
Ian Graham
ISBN: 978-1-907184-59-8

The Tudors
Jim Pipe
ISBN: 978-1-907184-58-1

Ireland
Jim Pipe
ISBN: 978-1-905638-98-7

Wales
Rupert Matthews
ISBN: 978-1-907184-19-2

Yorkshire
John Malam
ISBN: 978-1-907184-57-4

...y..., and you retain v...
...you, you are liable to be ch...
...th theft and punished.

There were two previous convic...
against Turner for theft and he was ...
sentenced to three months' hard lab...
The chairman (Mr B. J. Saunders, C.B...
said the prisoner may have made a g...
uine mistake in the first instance, but he h...
deliberately kept property which did not b...
long to him.

CASTLE ALTRUM

SENSATIONAL CHASE OVER ROOFS.

Altrum Village police are still looking for a
woman "cat" burglar who by her excep-
tional daring has escaped with a large haul
of literary works taken from the Cherish
Library at Castle Altrum, the Scottish home
of the Cherish family. The woman was
nearly captured by Mr Edgar Staples, the
butler, who discovered her in the library. He
ran after her into the grounds and followed
her when she dashed into a storeroom in
the stable block and made her way up onto
the roof. After clambering over the roofs
for some time the woman eluded her pur-
suer by sliding down a stack-pipe into an
overgrown area. Naturally, Mr Staples did
not have much chance of seeing the
woman, but she is described as being about
twenty-two years of age, and about 5ft.
2ins. or 5ft. 3ins. in height. She is slightly
built, and at the time of her discovery she
was wearing a dark costume coat and a
small, close-fitting hat. She escaped into the
night on a motorcycle, closely pursued by
Ajay Jasbir and Sanjay Jarrol, who were
guests of the Cherish family.